MW00635722

ROMANY MARIE

The Queen of Greenwich Village

to See & Betty Rout
we grew up together
in that Bohemian
orbit!

Bob Schulman
2006

Romany Marie

The Queen of Greenwich Village

Robert Schulman

BUTLER BOOKS

These tales centered around a remarkable woman are dedicated
to those who lived them and to those who helped evoke them.

First edition, July 2006

Editing and page design by Eric Butler

Butler Books
P.O. Box 7311
Louisville, KY 40207
502-897-9393
www.butlerbooks.com

ISBN 1-884532-74-8

Printed in Canada by Friesens Printers through
Four Colour Imports, Louisville, KY

Acknowledgments

As readers will realize early on, Romany Marie herself was the primary source for the contents of this volume. One of Marie's favorite activities was conversation. She had a marvelous gift for literate and sensitive expression, plus a considerable sense of recall that was often touched by insight as well as diplomacy. Over a period of several years, she generously unrolled these gifts in tapings which I made with her.

Among other sources, many of Marie's patrons were immensely helpful in interviews. Among them was Jan Yoors, a celebrated chronicler of Romany whose friendship with Marie attested to his respect for her gypsy persona.

The weekly *Village Voice*, a recorder of Village doings and personalities since 1955, provided important material—notably the Marie impressions by author Katherine Anne Porter. Other information and comment about Village history, mores and personalities came from the following:

Millay in Greenwich Village by Anne Cheney; *John Sloan, A Painter's Life* by Van Wyck Brooks; *The Improper Bohemians* by Allen Churchill; *Art Young, His Life and Times* edited by John Nicholas Beffel; and *My Life and Loves in Greenwich Village* by Maxwell Bodenheim.

Also, *Theodore Dreiser* by F.O. Matthiessen; *Revolutionary Lives (Anna Strunsky and William English Walling)* by James Boylan; *Greenwich Village, Culture and Counterculture* edited by Rick Beard and Leslie Cohen Berlowitz; and *Greenwich Village, A Guide to America's Legendary Left Bank* by Judith Stonehill.

Other kinfolk of Marie's—Lee Rout, Valerie and Christopher Rout, Romanie Rout (named in tribute to Marie) and the late William Morris Abbott—contributed rare memorabilia and unmatched support; also Eleanor Langham and Louise Tachau Schulman.

Finally, this book might never have made it into print without the stubborn devotion manifested by Butler Publishing's president Bill Butler, who won a medical battle in order to continue his imaginatively edited output.

The Chapters

1. Entrance	11
2. Raised Among the Romanies	27
3. Marie Comes to New York	38
4. Starting Up in Greenwich Village	47
5. The First Center	61
6. Sasha Stone and Europe	78
7. The Lure of the Village	89
8. Bucky and Marie	104
9. A Colony of Artists	116
10. A Cast of Characters	131
11. "Dr." Marchand	152
12. Back in Action	174
13. The Queen is Dead	188

Sculptor-designer Isamu Noguchi (pointing) and architect-inventor "Bucky" Fuller. A 2006 exhibit at the Noguchi Museum focused on their long, productive friendship, formed and nurtured by Romany Marie in her Village bistro. *(Arnold Eagle photo, courtesy of Noguchi Foundation and Garden Museum)*

"They came—I'm in a position to know—they came to Greenwich Village from all parts of the country. Youngsters. Some were pseudos. Always, there are pseudos, escaping rather than truly searching, confusing wild sex and drinks with the totality of the truth. But the others, over coffee and 10-cent glasses of tea, talked, wrote, painted and sang of things that moved the world. They were things from which came many of the shining insights of today. In a place like mine, they had a center where they could exchange thoughts. That kind of center is always a need, and more today than ever."

—Romany Marie, 1959

"Eternal Villageance is the price of liberty."

—Bobby Edwards, 1924

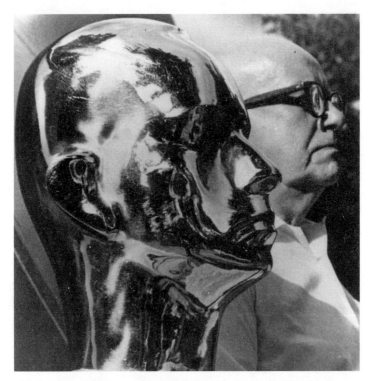

Buckminster Fuller posed in 1929 with a bust of him done by Isamu Noguchi after the two were first brought together at Romany Marie's, then on the Village's Minetta Street. A review in 1929 labeled it a "hot spot for creative types." *(Isamu Noguchi photo courtesy of Noguchi Foundation & Garden Museum)*

1. ENTRANCE

Early in the 20th century he was a floundering depressive. But by the century's close he was a world-renowned sage.

That was Buckminster Fuller.

As the 20th century ended, he was cited as having been perhaps the era's Leonardo da Vinci. After all, he had contributed the geodesic dome, the towered Dymaxion house and the turn-on-its-chassis Dymaxion car. He had created the concept of "Spaceship Earth," and had invented devices that anticipated automation and convenience in the American home. He had embraced architecture, engineering, mathematics, cartography, philosophy, poetry and cosmology. In 2004, he was honored with a U.S. postage stamp.

But in 1926, Fuller had been adrift in New York City's Greenwich Village, almost penniless, mocked for what were considered his loony ideas. He had even considered suicide.

The arresting contrast between those dismal beginnings and his later, formidable accomplishments was characteristic of what happened to many like Fuller in Greenwich Village before and after World War II. Those were the decades when rebellious American youth counted on being separate, in that southern segment of Manhattan island, from the millions of stuffy people elsewhere in the metropolis and beyond.

Fuller found his renewal and the gateway to his fame in the therapeutic boosts given him by the welcoming hostess of a little, Paris-type bistro located over a stationery store on the Village's Washington Square.

She called herself Romany Marie, and was later hailed in the neighborhood's weekly newspaper as the "Queen of Greenwich Village" and the last vestige of its true Bohemia. As Fuller said later, "She fed my belly and my psyche. My creative world was born in the world of Romany Marie."

What she did was give Fuller a home away from his donated, one-room flat, with free food and a place to talk. "The poor fellow, everybody loved him but nobody seriously wanted him or his ideas," said Marie, who had started her Village center in 1914, so much more devoted to her patrons than to any profit that, in her almost 40 Village years, she had to move her place ten times.

"Knowing my acute needs, Marie gave me a proposition, a free meal whenever I wished it," Fuller recalled. "Really, it worked out quite well because she had her great, thick beef-stock soup—her 'chorba'— with black bread, and prunes for dessert. But there was more. Marie said to me, 'I tell you what, you be my Official Talker. You come in as many nights as you can and talk to people.'"

It was exactly what he needed. Fuller mused, "Every intellectual in the world came in at one time or another. I argued and discussed endlessly with them, and purified my concepts. That is why I say my creative world was born in the world of Romany Marie."

From the beginning of the twentieth century up to the 1950s, "Bucky" Fuller's experience was paralleled in Greenwich Village by an astonishing throng later globally renowned in *belles lettres*, arts and entertainment.

For many of them, Romany Marie Marchand was a central personality, hailed often as a kind of earth mother. The Romanian sculptor Constantin Brancusi, artist Isamu Noguchi, whose lifelong friendship with Fuller began at Marie's, Burl Ives, film's Eddie Albert, comedians Danny Kaye and Zero Mostel, Catholic social activist Dorothy Day, those chroniclers of civilization Will and Ariel Durant, many of the century's explorers—these and many others all said Marie helped them momentously, in a special time and place, to find the touchstone to their eventual recognition and success.

The question is: does today's Greenwich Village remain such a special place for a special time?

After all, despite dramatic changes, the narrow, twisted streets and alleys and many of the quaint houses that give the Village its special ambiance are still there.

What's more, the centers of bold, inventive, breakthrough theatre, dance and art that used to be a Village monopoly are now found also in other New York neighborhoods, in the East Village and Soho, further south, even across New York's rivers, in Brooklyn and Queens. Some would say this is the old Village phenomenon tripled or quadrupled.

Yet most of those who lived through what the *Village Voice* newspaper often called the neighborhood's true Bohemia would argue that today the old, generative chemistry bubbles no longer.

In neighborhood after neighborhood, rapid economic change disperses the artists and writers to yet another section where low-grade, affordable quarters are quickly discovered and publicized, and the hunt for fresh digs resumes.

Typically, one such neighborhood transition was noted in a *New York Times* "Style" article in July 2004 about changes in lower Manhattan's old meat-packing district, described as a three-block-deep neighborhood below 14th Street at the Hudson River.

"Once a shadowy sanctum of transvestite prostitutes, leather bars and full-service poultry and beef providers, it is now restaurants, scene-y hotels and roped-off lounges. Limo drivers and magazine writers crowd the streets almost every night."

An old-time denizen cited the usual transition: "First the artists move, then the yuppies come in. And as soon as your favorite bar gets written up, it's all over."

One key change is that in the Village of yore, the rebellious, convention-busting young were not only looked upon by the mainstream as weird or morally dangerous; they themselves sanctified that separation.

"Eternal Villageance is the price of liberty," sang Bobby Edwards, a Harvard-spawned, bemused satirist who sold homemade cigar box ukuleles at Marie's in the 1920s. Recognition by the conventional community and by the "uptown" press was counted a sellout.

In 1917, in the same separatist spirit, painters John Sloan and Marcel Duchamp and other Marie habitués were key players who dramatized their opposition to U.S. involvement in World War I by a partying "take-over" of the Washington Square arch. They issued a pronouncement that declared the Village independent from the rest of New York and the nation, "a new territory of the mind and soul."

Nowadays, by contrast, some of the smallest off-off Broadway plays, ballets and art exhibits get ready recognition from *The New York Times* and other media. Book after book rolls out to proclaim that no separation remains any longer, that Bohemia has given way to "bobo"—bourgeois Bohemia.

Further, then-radical lifestyles that were exclusive to bohemian Villagers are now pursued everywhere. The embrace of extra-marital "free love," of what birth control pioneer Margaret Sanger as a Villager daringly espoused as "family limitation" and of minorities and homosexuals that used to be unique to the Village have now been accepted by much of the mainstream.

But perhaps the most significant Village change is the disappearance of "centers" (as she called them) like Romany Marie's. They were eating and talking places where as-yet undiscovered, creative characters rather than celebrities were the honored habitués, where most regulars were poor enough to exchange a painting or a song or a dance or a poem reading for a meal and could find an accepting place.

Beginning in 1910 or so, and continuing even up to 1950, there used to be clusters of such low-profit "centers" quartered in the dingy, dimly-lit but welcoming lofts and old flats on storied, crooked streets and alleys such as Christopher, Grove and the "Minettas"—street, lane, place and court.

But a myriad of remembrances by those who trace their career awakenings to Marie cite her and her places as the essence of what was the Village chemistry.

And what makes it compellingly contemporary is the degree to which so many of those graduates insist that it was the separation of their restless, challenging Village life from the commercial, more conventional parts of New York that fueled their creativity. Indeed, a handsome photo and text anthology about the Village published in 1993 still wistfully defined the Village as "continuing to be New York's most vibrant and tolerant district."

A lifelong friend of Bucky Fuller, the celebrated sculptor Isamu

Noguchi also held that view. Noguchi met Fuller at Romany Marie's in 1929. He had been directed there while serving as an assistant in Paris to Romanian-born Constantin Brancusi, himself an admirer and sometime guitar-strumming patron of Romany Marie's.

For Noguchi, Marie's café was what he called "a habitué." There, he said, many nights of exploring talk shaped his future years of portraits of the later-famous—such as Clare Boothe Luce, Ginger Rogers and playwright Thornton Wilder—in clay, aluminum, marble and wood. Later came his large, graceful sculptures that won a major retrospective exhibit in 1989, the widely heralded reopening of a Long Island sculpture garden in 2004, and a 2006 exhibit highlighting the Noguchi-Fuller friendship.

The same, lasting after-effect of early Village creators came with sculptor Brancusi. A 2004 exhibit of his works that took over all of Manhattan's circular Guggenheim Museum brought from *The New York Times* reviewer the conclusion that, like another ex-Villager also on view, Amadeo Mogdigliani, Brancusi's sculptures bridged "the gap between the Stone Age and the space age."

"Marie, Marie, Marie!"

Even now that tends to be the nostalgic way in which Marie devotees or contemporary lovers of the old Village voice their wistful longing for decades that may not now be revivable but plead to be remembered.

Can there come again, if not in New York or its outer borough extremities then elsewhere—in Philadelphia, Chicago, San Francisco, L.A. or even a Louisville or a Denver—one or more earth mothers like Romany Marie or her early parallel, Polly Holladay, giving individuals committed to what Marie called "a place for the searching to find themselves"?

Perhaps today's culture of total communication defies that option. If so, all the more reason to immerse ourselves in what Marie and other wellsprings of Bohemia helped make possible.

That village, that labyrinth of streets and lanes some two miles north of the tip of Manhattan island into which those restless individuals seeking political or social or cultural change began settling after 1910 consisted mostly of buildings grown dingy since prosperous New Yorkers had begun moving northward.

But cheap lodging was ideal for young change-seekers with little money and a yen for the unorthodox in sex, garb, and writing, painting, dancing or politicking. Further, the neighborhood proximity to Manhattan's lower East Side, home to recently arrived immigrants, made it a seedbed for those newcomers who grabbed for radical concepts that seemed to promise bringing to reality an idealist's view of America.

Marie was one of those newcomers. Migrating to the U.S. from rural Romania as a teenager, she worked as a sweatshop seamstress to bring her natural-healer mother and her three sisters and young brother to join her.

Their rapid command of English was helped by involvement in Socialist schools and workshops conducted by such personalities reported on by a scandalized mainstream as anarchist Emma Goldman and Will Durant, later a universally acclaimed historian, but then principal of a school named after an assassinated Spanish anarchist.

After piecework on coats and hats helped the family move upward to the city's borough of the Bronx, their home became such a favorite gathering place for intellectually and gastronomically hungry Village types that Marie boldly decided to make embracing hospitality a career.

"Our neighbors there in the Bronx would see all these people who looked strange to them and they would worry, they said we were 'different,'" Marie said later in one of many interviews. "Well, we were. You could sometimes hear for a block the arguments and the debates about violence and marriage and sex and discipline, and once one of the extreme anarchists"—Alexander Berkman, Emma Goldman's sweetheart—"even came to hide because the police were after him and wanted to question him.

"So, suddenly one night, several of our guests said why should they go on exploiting our home? It wasn't fair to come all that way from the Village to eat our food and drink our coffee. Why shouldn't I open a little place in the Village?"

Egged on even by several notorious spongers who reckoned that they might pay, Marie went for it, with $150 collected from various persons chipping in.

In 1914, Marie found what she called "a romantic place on the third floor of a funny building" which stood then on Washington Street at the corner of Sheridan Square.

She would make a center there, she said, based on the beautiful objective of the school named after anarchist Francisco Ferrer, "a center for people to get off the edge of dullness in their searching."

"Ferrer had said to love someone passionately is to have an ideal you will live and die for, and this center would be such an ideal. When some of the Wobblies from the IWW (a murderously revolutionary activist group) heard about it, they said they would break the place up." But Marie didn't worry, she felt they would be happy to call her place revolutionary "as soon as they got a taste." It was an obscure poet, David Ross, later a nationally known network radio announcer (Old Gold— mellow as a cello) but then a volunteer waiter, who persuaded her to call herself Romany Marie, in deference to the gypsies she always said she'd known in her childhood.

But while Marie's first bistro at 133 Washington Place drew its aficionados and did have a fireplace, it was reachable only by a flight of outside stairs and then two inside flights. And typical of many Village accommodations, it had a landlord sympathetic neither to Bohemians nor to late rental payments.

So in 1914 there began for Marie and her followers in the next four decades the succession of moves, each of them signaled by a handwritten note on the front door: The Caravan Has Moved.

To be sure, a factor in Marie's persistence as a low-profit entrepreneur was her gloriously colorful husband, Danon Marchand. A linguist, inventor, chiropractor and philanderer, his relationship with Marie was such that affairs by each of them never destroyed their love, which Marie said he signaled by calling it "Yontiff"—Yiddish for holiday— each time they had sex.

But through the years, as one patron said, Marchand's chief role was to make the tavern cockroaches run faster. Indeed, through all her Village years, Marie got frequent, though protesting, subsidies from her successful purse-manufacturing brother who tended to regard her artsy patrons as spongers.

Still, the economic marginalism was typical of many of the early Village cafés, even after the beginning surge of curious tourists.

So it was that after only a year, the Romany Marie Tavern had to move in 1915 to Number 20 Christopher Street. This proved to be a more fortunate location because Marie was able to stay there until 1923. It became the place of which John Sloan did an etching, a work that found a place in the permanent collection of New York's Metropolitan Museum of Art.

After that, for almost two years, Marie functioned at 170 Waverly Place, up only one flight of stairs and with two fireplaces. It was at the corner of Christopher Street, a mecca for gay men and lesbians years before a 1969 riot marked what was said to be the start of gay rights.

Marie's Waverly Place Tavern was followed by a Romany Marie Tavern in a location over the stationery store on Washington Square, in what had been the celebrated "Bruno's Garret," legendarily the early quarters for a public hangman.

Among the next seven locations, one briefly was at a second address on the Square, highlighted by an exciting but stormy partnership with historian Ariel Durant. Another, in 1929, at number 15 Minetta Street, was the occasion for an innovative but unstable aluminum furniture and lighting arrangement by Buckminster Fuller, and then a Fuller-designed printed announcement describing an art exhibit by Mark Tobey. It introduced that painter's "white" canvas concept which made him internationally famous thirty years later as winner of the Venice Biennale competition.

Like so many other of Marie's flock, Tobey was a prima donna whose eventual success heightened his sour moods. In 1951, *Life* Magazine's recognition of his artistic eminence drew from him only a bitter complaint that one of his abstract paintings had been published upside down. He never withdrew the charge, even though the magazine noted that the painting had been published with his signature at its bottom.

Yet the artist's misty-eyed devotion to Marie remained through the years, even from far-off Seattle where Tobey spent his later times, and where yet another Marie devotee, Zoe Dusanne, traced her founding of Seattle's first modern art gallery to her times at Marie's.

So it went with another longtime friend, Hutchins (Hutch) Hapgood, who by 1939 was a successful author and New York newspaper columnist. Hapgood wrote a book that year in which one Sadakichi Hartmann was dusted off as "a parasite."

This should not have occasioned any argument. Hartmann was never surpassed as the greatest sponger among literati of the twentieth century. Along with a gift for fathering exquisite poetry and a multitude of children, the beanpole-shaped Hartmann was able to beg, borrow or steal food, money and whiskey even from such redoubtable skeptics as fabled stage and screen comedian W.C. Fields and actor John Barrymore.

But when Hapgood's book appeared, Sadakichi's illness did not save him from a bristling challenge. To his bedside came a strong-featured woman in her mid-fifties, wearing a complex of green and purpled skirts, a colorful blouse and a velvet coat ornamented with gold mesh. Pendants hung from her neck and ears, and on her arms and fingers were exotic jades, onyxes and bronzes.

"How could you just call Sadakichi Hartmann a parasite?" she demanded of the startled Hapgood. "Is it because you have money and Hartmann doesn't? So he did ask for handouts now and then, so what? How could you put him down with one unpleasant title when Sadakichi is, as Walt Whitman would say, a multitude of personalities?"

As she rustled off, she muttered in what Hapgood later was said to have observed as a husky voice that would put a testosterone tenor to shame, that the trouble with the world was the judging of people by only one shadow.

It was, of course, Romany Marie. Out of her childhood in her native Romania she brought a kind of earth mother insight that arranged first opportunities for budding young talents, sent the weak backpacking home, and brooked little patience for those who couldn't see some good in almost everybody, if properly manipulated.

Mainstream America always regarded with leery uneasiness (and morbid curiosity) the places where its new young writers and poets and painters gathered to stand on their heads in protest against conventional ways. From at least 1900 until even after World War II, Greenwich Village was that place.

But nowadays, the few remaining alumni of that old Village look askance at new "Village" shifts and the quick media embrace of untested, experimental art forms. That, most of them say, shows a poverty of judgment from which "their" Village never suffered.

Unarguably, one difference was that their Village had Romany Marie—and what is a healthy Bohemia without Mother? The theme of her life and the crux of her influence was her passionate determination not to be in the restaurant business primarily for profit. In this she succeeded admirably, spending her last years almost in dependent penury. But this hardly bothered her, even at the bitter end. Romany Marie was more concerned with what she rightly saw as her mission: to keep a place where, along with her Romanian chorba to warm the insides, the searching and the questing people could warm their spirits in a lingering tempo, and take from her sixth-sense intuitions what they needed in coddling or flailing to find their way.

In this she succeeded so strikingly that upon her death in 1961 she was mourned as the Godmother of the Village. "La Reine" they called her. Also, essence friend. In a milieu of razor wit and restless, rebellious ego, she was genial humor and helpfully pithy humor. *"Oh, Marie ... Marie ... Marie!"*—from Madrid to Mexico City, there came the litany with which so many used to greet her upon returning to the Village after a long absence. Monroe Wheeler, a director of New York's Museum of Modern Art, said, "Marie picked you up when luck was running low and she intensified joy when luck was running high. She loved the little ones as much as the great ones, and she wrote a vital page in our cultural history."

Once, Marie prevailed upon one of her better-heeled patrons to give overnight shelter to the appropriately pale, sonnet-writing lover of Lola Ridge, a beatnik poet of some note in the 1920s. Two days later, the patron reported angrily to Marie that his guest, upon departing, had taken his benefactor's overcoat. "I'm amazed you should be so petty," Marie exclaimed. "You have a nice, warm place while he has only the overcoat. Someday his poems will sell and he will make it up to you."

She did not mind at all being bossy about expressed needs. When a longtime friend, the French-born Edgar Varese, was just beginning to lead in composition of atonal, electronic music, he appeared one night in 1932 at Marie's place, despondent over his lack of critical acceptance. "Varese, what is wrong with you?" Marie cried, looking at the handsome Frenchman over the boiling soup pot. "People can say there is no music in the gurgling of this pot, but sooner or later their appetite will awaken them to the music!" Many years later, in his garden-court studio in the Village, Varese remembered. He tapped one of the dozens of vari-colored metal strips hanging over his worktable. "She crystallized all colors, she charged our batteries while she challenged the weak or the phony," he said. "It was smelling people and feeling people. Right away, she had something on you—like a loving animal."

Marie herself recalled the early occasion when Theodore Dreiser, the bestseller novelist of the 1920s and 1930s, came to her place. He sipped eight cups of her Turkish coffee and announced that he was working on a book about artists that became *The Genius*. Marie, hearing about his desire to savor the atmosphere of an artist's studio, sent him to the Sixth Avenue loft-studio of her friend John Sloan, one of the early century's American art titans whose peppery wife, Dolly, was also a Marie aficionado. "Sloan is the warmest and most human of all the painters," Marie said she told Dreiser.

But according to Van Wyck Brooks' later biography of Sloan, Dreiser found the Sloan studio too devoid of gimcracks to suit his novelist tastes; he went on to create an artist character in his book whose liking for luxury and cavalier conduct with women offended Sloan. Marie chided Sloan: "You should remember that Dreiser is a difficult one to like and to understand. And he has told me that the part of the story that is about you is the admirable part—the enthusiasm to paint the saloons and the El trains and the real people of the city." Marie felt thereafter that this became a factor in Sloan's verve for at least a few other of the bulky Dreiser novels.

An unashamed matchmaker ahead of her time (with no particular espousal of marriage), Marie made a tall girl who had been one of the many Dreiser sweethearts the object of one of her romantic campaigns. By then, the girl had been married and divorced from Howard Scott. "Like a tall Indian," Marie described Scott, who had spent so much time in Marie's restaurants developing his role as the "father" of the Technocracy movement, widely popular in the depression 1930s, that he laughingly called Marie the "mother" of technocracy.

"She had a terribly unhappy time with Scott," Marie said of the young woman, "a stunning and versatile brunette" named Kyra Markham. "There she was trying to develop her talents as an actress and writer, and he was mentally knocking her down while trying to develop his." After the divorce, Marie spent almost a year maneuvering to get the girl together with a young stage designer by telling him that, after Dreiser and Scott, the girl felt this unassuming young unknown to be a bore.

One night they came to Marie with their marriage license, announcing to her, "This is a marriage you made." Said Marie later, "She developed like a flower. I knew it would work because she'd had her try with big shots, she was now ready for a marriage where she could be the God."

But there were a multitude of other occasions throughout the years when Marie, judging that some young patron was merely drifting toward trouble, would persuasively convince her to return home—to that rest of the nation that Marie persistently summarized as "Oshkosh or Hodge Podge." To a celebrated photographer in the 1930s who was blocking such a homeward return Marie delivered a verbal laceration: "You talk anti-Semitic but you like a Jewish girl in bed. Why don't you become consistent? Stick with one and let the other go!"

Not that anyone ever called Marie a blue-nose about sex. Her morality on this score in Bohemia was that sex was to be questioned only when disproportionately stressed. Her categorical stands did come against drunkenness in her restaurants, regardless of the fame of the drinker. Accordingly, she was steamingly affronted in the late Prohibition era when the local precinct police captain walked in one night to tell her she must begin paying a fee for extra protection. "Protection from what?" she asked, hands on hips over swirling gypsy skirts. The policeman said leeringly, "Protection from raids for liquor on the premises." Marie cried, "For that I need no protection!"

She stepped away and whispered to actor-writer Harrison Dowd, who in 1924 had brought the then-Prince of Wales to her place, and who on this occasion was happily accompanied by the brother of then-New York Mayor Jimmy Walker. The moment the police captain digested this fact, he shouted to a subordinate who was poking around in Marie's kitchen, "Murphy! Let's beat it."

It was neither the first nor the last of Marie's scrapes with officialdom. She established her first haven when Greenwich Village still had "village" characteristics and through the next 35 years, while the Village changed, Marie struggled to retain the atmosphere of gypsy rusticity, pleasing "her" people but giving ulcers to health, fire and safety inspectors. An outdoor, Chic Sale toilet, reachable only by descending three stories down an iron staircase, constituted sanitary facilities for the place where Marie began, in a Village still rich in old houses with steep slate roofs, chimney pots and small framed windows. To reach her places, patrons almost always had to walk way up, or way down. Marie stuck exclusively to candlelight until inspector's screams forced her surrender to electricity. From her location in the late 1920s, diners could smell the odors of the old livery stable next door. No help to antiseptic cleanliness were her wooden tables, dust-catching draperies and copper pots, and her liking for meats broiling in an open stone fireplace.

No help, either, were the great accumulations of books, papers and chemicals that came, along with high camp insults, from Marie's husband, Danon, whose walrus mustache and forest-thick hair on a leonine head always made him look like one of Marie's more rebellious patrons.

Marie's spirit and food held the chemistry all together; the only change in décor she ever allowed came on that late 1920s occasion when she yielded to the suggestion of an impoverished "Bucky" Fuller to aluminize and illuminate the place. There ensued such a comical disruption of the Romany Marie atmosphere that it made some of the New York papers.

Typically, as recounted, Marie continued to befriend Fuller. So a half century later, when at a posh 1967 gathering in Seattle in his honor somebody mentioned to Fuller Marie and the Village, the stubby little super-scientist snapped to like a swain seeing his beloved come out of a mist.

"Marie, Marie, Marie!" Fuller exclaimed, forgetting everyone else in the room. "She was a Vesuvius of creativity in heart and mind. She had all kinds of friends, but she harbored such a powerful, simpatico drive that she could soul-feed all of us, usually several at the same time in concurrent conversations."

To her role of providing food and earthy philosophy Marie brought what she maintained were the values of having grown up among romanies—gypsies. This occasioned periodic sniping in her own circles as well as from the unknowing uptown, even though she always readily acknowledged she was no gypsy. Teddy Ballantine, a key figure in the Provincetown, Massachusetts theatre that launched Eugene O'Neill, and later a pioneer in paperback book publishing, would josh Marie upon coming in to find her amid her restaurant flock.

"Mitten derinnen!" he would shout—Yiddish for in the middle of it all. With her enveloping laugh, Marie would respond, "Du bist a zeesa Goy!"—You're a sweet Gentile.

Less congenial was one early Village historian, Albert Parry, who gave Marie an obscure press notice that tended to be typical. "Romany Marie, a Romanian Jewess, used to be an ardent Anarchist usher at Emma Goldman's meetings," he wrote, "but scared by the anti-Red campaign of the World War I period, she now went into the crazy jinks tearoom business in the Village. She posed as a gypsy, she introduced colorful trappings, fortune telling and gypsy music into the Village."

But quite apart from the fact that Marie's cadre of patrons included not only anarchists but Wobblies, Socialists, Communists and Vegetarians, likening her to a tearoom operator was, for her, like accusing her of streetwalking. More, the rich color of her Old World tales had living witness from her cigarette-smoking mother.

Esther Yuster was an herb-healer, weaver and concocter of entrancing dishes. It was from her knowledge of the ways of gypsies and of nature, rather than from adaptive insight, that Marie said her own sharp intuitions came. A testimonial to one of these, Marie's knack of reading the grounds in a cup of Turkish coffee came from Edith Halpert, longtime operator of a major, mid-Manhattan art gallery and until the 1960s a doyenne of the American art world.

Miss Halpert had brought Nelson Rockefeller to Marie's long before his entry into politics and emergence as a state and national figure. He was introduced to Marie as Mister Nelson. But when she read his cup, she said, "I see in the background hills of gold ..." Once a fascinated Rockefeller could be spirited outside by his companion, she eyed him bemusedly. "Evidently you're going to be a rich man."

On another occasion an officer of the Chicago Art Institute brought with him to Marie's a Negro philosophy professor whom the Chicagoan knew to be a homosexual. "He was no pinkie-fluttering simperer, he was a real guy, but within ten minutes of their first talking Marie had him spotted," the Chicagoan said. "The thing is, the way she treated it gave him a terrific lift and made them fast friends." Marie shrugged later, "It was nothing magnanimous. I could simply sense that here was a man who was turning his lack of normal sex into constructive thinking, and I told him so. I call such a man a homogenius."

In 1939, when Marie was having more trouble than usual even for her in meeting the landlord at the door, 300 persons of high and low estate assembled at the Villagers' favorite hostelry, the since-demolished Brevoort, for a testimonial benefit dinner calculated to keep Marie in business. The organizer, Joseph Robinson of the New York Explorers' Club, said, "Close Romany Marie's and for many of us you may as well close the Village." Marie got up and, without even waiting for word of the proceeds, rapped the podium. "I will not close," she said. "The old girl is still with you!"

"Old" for her, at 54, was a uniquely ill-chosen adjective. Twenty years later, at 74, she was still at it, although by then devoid of her own restaurant and functioning as a sort of reigning Character in Residence. One night in 1959 she appeared on a radio talk show, and from midnight to 5 a.m. regaled her audience with homilies. One was that it was desirable for some creative young girls to have affairs but that others would do well to remain pure.

A week later, a young admirer joined her on one of her daily strolls through the Village. I was that admirer—her nephew, with many hours of Marie recollections on (wire) tape to give me, a Bronx boy, a sense of the world, which I had only marginally enjoyed.

These strolls of hers gave passing tourists the impression that they were seeing a genuine bohemian. Her expressive hands, the curve of breasts that had been spared much of the sagging effects of time. Her graying hair was strikingly piled in a double pompadour with a rose for accent. Her garments and accessories were of storied source—a French jacket from writer Will Durant and his wife Ariel (sometimes called "Puck"), a fur stole from Cissie Patterson of the newspaper clan. A handsome amethyst brooch had come from Princess Henrietta Savaggio, a former lady-in-waiting to Romania's Queen Marie, whom Marie had first befriended when the displaced princess reached New York to become a writer and painter.

Marie told her young companion on the walk that she'd used her special healing methods to tackle a throat problem before a radio program. "Imagine, I knew I would need my voice for the radio thing, but on the night before, I couldn't even say moo. So I said to the good in myself which I call God, 'I need my voice tomorrow.' Then I gargled ten times with salt and hot water. And when I awakened the next morning, the voice was booming. Imagine!" Again, that deep, enveloping laugh.

The program had brought her calls from all manner of devotees. "You know what I am to them?" she said. "I'm a legend. I'm an idea. Many times, when such people get together, the thing to do is to talk about me and to reminisce. Where they started, how their work began. Oh yes, they'll say, was that in Marie's Washington Square place, or in the one on Christopher Street? They can scarcely speak of their past without bringing in one of my centers, for that is what my places were— not so much restaurants as centers for people to get off the edge of the ordinary."

Marie said, "A man would be working furiously on a piece of music. Another would be writing for ten hours. Still another would be faking, looking for escape into sex and drift but calling it 'art' or 'revolt' to justify it. They would come to me with their enthusiasm, or with their discord—Marie, why has this been such a bad day for me? Marie, why can't I find a belief in mankind? Perhaps I could be a source for such people because, unlike a recording machine, I would react with my whole being, for I, too, was in the act of creation and that was the real food."

She continued, "Where else could they find such a thing? At a bar, where everybody mouths nothingness, pats the other person on the behind and screams, 'Let's have another drink and get stinking'? The great thing is to know what you are, what your particular nature is. I myself have never painted or written or danced. But I have had my medium, and it has been enriching for me. My medium has been people—a very hard medium because there are moods and bellyaches and disturbances. But human, human, always human."

2. Raised Among the Romanies

As a girl in Romania, she loved most the fields and the green shadows of the woods, where the gypsies camped.

Often, she went onto one of the little paths leading up the vineyards, where she could lie on her back in the sun and let grapes fall into her mouth.

"I spent hours studying how the grape grows," she said. "Watching the birds. Watching how things develop in the spring. Other times I sat among the gypsies, watching them work, watching them play. Mother did not keep me from them. She served the gypsies, and the peasants, too, in the little inn and general store we had on the outskirts of the forest. She knew them. 'They are not saints,' she said to me. 'But they have a high morality.'"

As for the gypsies themselves, they liked this lively, daring little girl with the blooming, robust figure and the dark, vivid face.

"Your red, red dimpled cheeks are like two stones," they told her. "Solid." They sensed her love of nature and enjoyed the way she sat among them for hours at a time.

She watched them carve, hammer and mold almost all the objects they needed for everyday living. In open fires they baked dishes fashioned out of lumps of clay. Their spoons were made of wood, and intricately designed. They created beautifully-formed copper pots and pitchers.

Many of them danced or played one-string violins. And their lovemaking went on openly, without self-consciousness.

All this the girl drank up. Soon the Jews in the village disapprovingly began to call her "Meschiunka": Little Gypsy.

"I don't care," she said defiantly. "I've got dimples, and when I comb my hair, I look nice."

She was the pushy child in the family. And the happiest, she said, because she did not feel the compulsion always to be good.

"One night," she said, "I climbed up and spent the whole night in our cherry tree. I had a happy time, eating the blossoms. They're very sweet, you know. Meanwhile, Mother and my sister, Rebecca, went running around frantically looking for me. I knew I was in for trouble. I had let the goat into the garden, and the feather pillows for the swing were all chewed up. 'If I'm gone all night,' I said to myself, 'they will be so happy to see me they'll forget what I've done. And so it was.'"

But one day her mother decided it was time for the girl to begin learning the finer aspects of sewing, so she could be of more help at home. "She sent me into the town, to be a seamstress' apprentice," Marie recalled. "I had a small room with a clay floor. My little heart burned so with homesickness that I decided to do something desperate."

Anything unimportant, she thought, and her mother would say, "No, you must finish what you've begun."

So she played dead. In vain, the seamstress tried to force food down her throat. She lay motionless and stiff on the clay floor, breathing only when nobody was looking. "In my little head, I planned it, I will stay that way until I hear Mother's voice and then I will cry out for her."

They sent for her mother, who was an overnight's journey away by horseback. She came, in a torrential downpour. When she entered the room, Marie whispered, "Take me out! Quickly!" The moment she had gotten Marie outside, into the rain, the girl put a hand gently across her mother's mouth.

"Don't scold me," she said softly. "I only died because I missed you."

Marie continues the story in her own words:

My father was a despot. His name was Lupo Yuster. Lupo means wolf, and never was a man more rightly named. He lured my mother into marriage on false premises. But he was a tall and handsome despot and all his life, from the time she met him, my mother loved him.

Her name was Esther Rosen, one of 13 children of a sage in the Romanian village of Rachitosa—the Place of Roots. She and a sister were the only two among all the 13 to live past puberty. As a result, their father kept them like flowers in a greenhouse, for fear that exposure to the juices of life would steal them away.

They were living in a house in town when Lupo came into my mother's life. She was 18, a beautiful, slender girl with raven hair and bright eyes.

Lupo came into the village from his inn in the forest, where he catered to farmers and peasants and gypsies. He was a refugee from Russia, a widower who had been married to a girl from Jassy. To everybody with whom he talked, along the way from his inn to the village, he said he owned most of the land around his inn.

As he passed by Esther's house, he looked up and saw her at the window. And she saw him.

That was it. He stopped in to see her father and a meeting was arranged. Presently, her father called Esther in. Lupo was in the room. "This man asks your hand in marriage," her father said. It was the first man who ever had had the chance to show an interest in Esther. Lupo was six feet two, dark and erect.

"Yes!" she exclaimed.

"But he has three children by his first marriages," her father said.

"That's all right, too," she said, "I love children!"

Lupo said, "She will be like a fourth child to me. I will treat her like a piece of jewelry."

Not until they were married did the truth come out. Lupo owned no land. He only wanted somebody to help run the inn.

I remember the many times when he struck her. Many times, while he ate, she would be out under the tree in the garden, weeping. He made her start smoking cigarettes, to show his mastery. But in his own tyrannical way, he loved her. And out of her trials came such a great person as I have never met. A person from whom I was still drawing wisdom when she died at 86.

She became not only innkeeper, wife and mother, but doctor and banker for the peasants and the gypsies.

I can recall, when I was only three, seeing Mother with a white bandanna on her black hair—she seemed very beautiful—carrying jugs of wine to the patrons at the tables, in a room so thickly-smoked you could cut it with a knife.

A one-string violin played, right through the smoke. We had a brick and clay oven, filled with fire, and on top of the oven all we children sat and watched the whole thing. And, every so often, the men would swing me down. "Come," they cried, "see how it is to dance with a gypsy!"

They went out into the fields to get for Mother little blossoms and herbs, and each plant she made into a medicine.

She put some in alcohol, some in olive oil, and then she applied them as healings when people were sick. Peasants came knocking at the inn door all the time for remedies.

"I have a cut," a big peasant said, holding out his arm. And this slender woman nodded her head and went to get a certain type of little blossom drowned in olive oil. She applied the remedy and bandaged the wound and in no time at all the injury healed.

Other times, it would be a pain in the stomach—something like what we here call appendicitis. She would take another plant or herb and give the person a drink of the mixture, and the trouble would pass.

In that primitive area where we lived, the only other doctor we had was an old monk.

He had an institution nearby to which sick and crippled people— and some dizzy people, too—were brought from all over Romania. And whenever this monk was called to the home of a sick person and found Mother at the bedside, he would say, "You don't need me."

Mother drew other knowledge from nature. In the fall, around our inn, it became like a beehive. A big fire blazed as preparations went on for the winter, when we all hibernated because of the terrible cold.

Mother operated on capons. Opening them up and doing the necessary cutting and then sewing the birds up again—Mother handled it just like a surgeon. As a result, all the neighbors brought her this work to do.

With the great fire burning, she made jellies and things, and the way she did them was out of this world. Into the basement she took sand by the bushel, and in it buried the most marvelous apples and pears. All winter, we could put in a hand and take out a fresh fruit. She made wine, and in the garret she hung her smoked salmon and other smoked delicacies.

Many came to watch, because what other young girls had in theory in their heads, she was putting into practice.

I remember the first spring I noticed her taking out a little box of seeds. But they were more than seeds, they were silkworms ready to be encouraged to build cocoons. And she did it right in the house, like baking a cake. She laid the little worms out on tables, and when they grew large, she brought in armsfull of mulberry leaves and laid them over the worms.

They ate themselves into sleepiness and began to make cocoons and then, before we knew it—we were children watching her—she was drawing, out of the yellow and white masses, strands of silk which she later put on a loom to make material. In the same artful way, she took wool from the sheep to make thread for our clothes.

She had a magic touch. On days when she made strudel dough, she stood at the table and said, "Look!" And she blew under the dough to test its fineness, and it fluffed up into the air and came floating down like a gossamer parachute.

All this she did while Lupo tyrannized her. She was not banal in any way. Always, she was alert and alive to the situation before her. Many times, Lupo would almost tear her hair out in the back room, and she would come out as if nothing had happened.

And out of all the children, she said, I was the closest to her because I was happiest. She said to me one day, "This is because I was the happiest when I was carrying you." I believe what a mother does during pregnancy influences the child, and so it was that Mother gave to me some of her happiness, her love of life and people.

Rebecca came first—she was the quiet and dependable child, and the sad one because she felt a pressure to be good. Then I came, on May 17, 1885, and afterward auburn-haired Rose and, finally, little David.

What Mother knew! The silk-making. And the medicinal things. And the way she kept the harvest money for the peasants, carrying on all their business in her head, without once taking a pencil in her hands—

these things she did not learn in school. She learned them from the old people, from those who had lived long, long years. She put her life to watching them, so she could soak in the traditions that came so naturally to her.

This is the way she led me to learn. Except for reading and writing, in a primitive school attended by the grown-ups as well as the children, I never had anybody pump knowledge into me. Maybe because my mother was so busy, it was my good fortune to be left to myself a great deal. I was free to take my knowledge from nature, from the woods and the people around me, clear and free to find what it was in my nature to find.

Where I was brought up, it could have been like a desert. It was for some. The people I grew up with were silent people. The peasants believed in exchange of products, in bartering without speaking. The women filled their aprons to their bosoms with eggs and vegetables and came to point, they'll take this and that and a little of this. Mother had such exchanges with them. For somebody who didn't have zest and life inside of them it could have been like a desert.

But I loved it, in spite of what Lupo was doing to Mother. In the worst traumatics, I had the happiest childhood a girl could have. Mother said, "It is because you take nature and nature takes you." The whole phenomenal panorama of life there, she said, was reaching me because for some reason I was conceived to be a part of it.

Beginning with early childhood, you need to fashion little vistas. Children get things from smell, hearing, taste—each of these forms is a source. All of a sudden, when the child grows up, he can find the vistas are there.

My vistas were in the change of the seasons, in birds and animals and growing things and the naturalness of the gypsies.

And in Mother. One night, in our wilderness, a fat woman, a friend of Mother's, came to visit. She wore a big skirt with pockets. The day she came, there was a big storm.

That night, there was a bright moon and the snow crunched when you walked on it. I went to the outhouse and on the way I saw this thing sparkling in the snow. It was a beautiful, little green box.

For me it was a piece of treasure. Quickly, I hid it under two buckets of ashes and snow. The next day, the fat woman came back all excited.

"Have you seen a little green box?" she asked Mother. It is her most precious possession, the woman says, and it has been lost—or stolen.

Stolen! Immediately, it gripped my heart, the fat woman will think I stole it!

Mother asked me, "Have you seen a little green box?" I turned my eyes away and said, "No."

All day I ached to tell her the truth, but I was afraid to. I roamed about, I walked in the woods, but there was a bad taste to it. When I could no longer stand it, I dug up the box and brought it to Mother.

"Look," I said. "I've found the fat woman's box."

That could have ended it, but I couldn't keep the secret.

"Mother?" I said. I held her arm and looked into eyes that seemed to guess what I was going to say, and made it a little easier. "I've had the box hidden away." And I told her how it had all happened.

Then things were right again between her and me. One thing she put into me very deeply: face the truth, tell no lies either to others or to yourself.

That day, she also cured me of remorse. It was a lesson for the future on how to ease a person's inner conflicts.

It was from Mother—and from the gypsies—I learned how to read, in the grounds of a cup of Turkish coffee, the things that many people need in order to face the future more realistically, or more cheerfully.

"This is not meant for everybody to do," one of the gypsy women told me one day. "You have to have an intuition to know what to say."

They pointed out figures in the cups, and lines. They said when such a figure comes near such a line, you use it as a springboard for beginning to see what you feel about a person whose cup you are reading.

Years later, it made me laugh inwardly, to have people ask me to teach them how to do it. Things like that you can't teach. You do it if you develop a sixth sense.

What is a sixth sense? It is what comes to a person who learns to face everything beyond the immediate problem. To discover out of the broader examination, by intuition, what to do for the immediate situation. A door opens, there is a way to go on.

There were many among the peasants and gypsies of my childhood who had this. Mother had it. The one place where she could not make it help was with Lupo—perhaps because she so loved him.

Out of the darkness of his own torments, he was forced to try to be a despot toward us girls as he was toward Mother. He was opposed even to our letting our hair grow. Fridays, we would all wash and braid our hair. One Friday, he caught me and cut my braids off.

"Too much freedom!" he shouted.

But a full measure of freedom was of nature, and in my nature. I made up my mind that someday I must find a way to get Mother away from Lupo—and get my brother and sisters free of him too, if I could manage it.

That is why I did not let myself go when I felt myself falling in love with any gypsy boy. That was not always easy.

There was one in particular. We went wandering far into the woods one day, and I got very hungry. And when I get hungry, all I want is meat.

I said to him, "Can't you go steal a chicken somewhere and broil it for me over a fire?" But there were no chickens in that wilderness. What did he do but take out his knife and bare his leg. He made like he wanted to cut a piece out of the calf of his leg and broil it for me.

I said, "No, no, no! I don't eat that kind of meat!"

But that's romance for you. I remember I went home to Mother and said, "I'll never go with a gypsy boy again. He wanted to give me flesh from his leg to eat."

She smiled and said, "Did you really fight him away from doing it?"

I was hardly more than 13 when I decided how I would rescue her from Lupo. I would arrange to go to America and earn the money to bring her after me. There, I heard, women were more than pieces of property to be used by men.

I had a girlfriend, also the daughter of an innkeeper, who was already there. I wrote her that if she would help me pay out for a steamship ticket, which you could get for less than fifty cents a week, I would like to come. Only Mother shared my secret.

Meanwhile, there were little ways I could use to square things with Lupo. For example, there was a gypsy whom the others called a doctor. He went around with a trained bear. He treated certain aches and pains by having the patient lie on his stomach. While the gypsy beat time on a drum, the bear would dance up and down on the patient's spine.

Lupo used to have the gypsy and his bear coming to the house every week. He couldn't live without it because when he was young, some bandits had caught him in the field and given him a terrible beating. He was a mean man, and they had it in for him. They left him with something injured in his back, and he felt it was the gypsy bear that kept him going.

When the bear didn't appear, he let me do it because I was a solid little girl. And whenever I got the chance to dance on his spine, I really jumped with all my weight, and every jump made me feel a little better.

One day he cried after me, "I don't like the way you walk down the street!"

It was a cruel thing to say because, although my figure was already developed, I was not conscious of my looks.

We were living, by then, outside the gates of Berlad. We would get up at five o'clock in the morning to help Mother prepare meals for peasants coming into town with their produce. Berlad, though still small, was one of the largest towns in Moldavia. It had sidewalk cafés and a public garden where on Thursday afternoons everybody shut up their businesses and came, dressed Parisian-like.

Music played in the garden, and the people promenaded and sat out in the cafés. I loved those days. Perhaps because I was a natural girl and came from the woods, I never put on a corset. I wouldn't cramp myself. And yet there wasn't a time when I didn't enjoy myself. I didn't feel that looks or figure had anything to do with drinking in the sights or the joy of being with people.

When Lupo raged at me about the way he thought I walked, I told him what I thought of his dictatorship. "My one hope is to get Mother free of you!" I cried. "What way is that to talk to the one who brought you into the world?" he shouted.

I answered, "You weren't doing anything for me. Only for your own pleasure!" I had seen the gypsies making love and making babies. I knew they did it in joyousness.

"If you had had to knock on a wall in order to bring me into the world," I told him, "you wouldn't have bothered!"

I already had my steamship ticket, sent to me by my friend in America, the day Betrinov came to the house. He was the handsomest thing God ever created. He was a middleman for handling grain. He looked like something painted by an Old Master—blue eyes, brown hair, reddish beard and a magnificent, six-foot stature.

He was a free-thinking man who said icons were symbols of fear. We talked there together, that afternoon, for five hours. I never had known a man with such thoughts. As for him I suppose it startled him to be engaged in such conversation with a 15-year-old girl.

That evening, he told Lupo he wanted to marry me. Not really as a wife, but to help me develop, to send me to Dresden to be educated.

In the night, lying in my bed, I heard Lupo excitedly waking Mother up. "Esther! Esther!" he said. "The grain dealer with the beard wants to marry Marie. Betrinov wants to marry Marie."

I heard my mother answer calmly, "That's for Marie to decide."

"For her to decide?" Lupo shouted. "What does she know? Since when does a girl decide what she is to do with her life? It's for us to decide."

A little later, Lupo came to my room. I made like I was asleep. He woke me and we talked. I thought of my steamship ticket. I evaded answering by saying I would give Betrinov my answer myself, in the morning.

When morning came, I arranged to be alone with Betrinov, and I showed him my passage to America. He was amazed, he wanted to know where such a girl could get a ticket to America.

I told him how I had managed it, and what it meant to me. Then he said, "I will send you to America!"

I said, "No, nobody is going to send me anywhere. I must go on my own. I must be free."

He was a man with understanding. When I wouldn't take money from him, he said, "Look, I have already been out shopping for a trousseau for you. Let me at least give you the things you need to travel with."

In those days, when girls traveled, they wore a lot of veiling around their hats. He fitted me out with the veiling and a beautiful traveling outfit and a set of fine valises.

As I look back, the fabrics were very fine. There was even a traveling coat, made of a material that was good for roughing it and for dressy times, too.

When Betrinov got through doing for me, I looked like a million dollars—but I had in my pockets only ten dollars more than I would need for the journey. A queen with an empty purse.

Lupo raged when he discovered my plans, but he couldn't stop me. America lay ahead.

I wasn't afraid. When I said goodbye to Mother, I told her, "I'll find a circle of people I can love. I'll see that they are the kind who think and feel; such people need not be feared. And then if I stumble and fall, it will be a soft fall because I'll be in my circle."

For the very beginning, I could count on my girlfriend, and on my oldest half-sister, Blema, who was also in America by then.

I had forgotten the man whom I had met one day when he came riding into our village with his company of the queen's cavalry. He was a fellow thirteen years my senior, an awesome and yet fascinating sight, with a bristling mustache and sideburns and dressed in a red tunic, white breeches and high boots.

I was to meet him again in New York. His name was Danon Marchand.

3. Marie Comes to New York

A room on New York's teeming East Side. A job in a sweatshop, usually to do piecework. Enrollment in night school to learn English. These were the elements in the customary pattern for immigrants arriving in New York in 1901.

Marie followed the pattern, but only up to a point.

Her half-sister, Blema, met her at the boat and took her to her East Side flat on Allen Street. Marie hauled her gift finery and the rest of her belongings into a dark, windowless bedroom.

That night, she sat on the bed and wrote to her mother: "It is an elegant street, mother dear. The elevator trains even run right outside the house!"

Next day she met with her girl friend. Through her, Marie was signed up to line coats on a piecework basis for a cloak factory.

"It is a little embarrassing, but I understand that in America it is an honor to do work—any kind of work," Marie said. "And I certainly can sew! I will take the hop!"

Within a few weeks, Marie was finishing as many as five or six coats a day, in addition to those she took home to work on while she talked.

Soon, she moved in with her friend, who was one of ten girls accommodated by a parsimonious woman who rented out space in a large apartment.

"Tell the girl it is our rule that no lights can burn after ten o'clock at night!" the landlady warned Marie's friend, shaking a stiff finger in Marie's direction.

That interfered with Marie's determination to write at least one letter a day to her mother. To solve it, she went out every night and wrote her letters by the glow of the street light.

She had two clear and immediate goals. One was to establish a home and earn enough money to send for her mother and the other children. The other was to learn the language and find her "circle of thinking people."

Preparing for the time when she could rent an apartment, she discovered it was possible to begin getting a set of furniture for 50 cents a week.

"New York is not altogether an unnatural place," she wrote her mother. "No matter how young a girl is, even as young as I am, if you go with proof that you are working, they trust you on anything. So it will not be long!"

Meanwhile, to learn English and to find her "circle," Marie resisted enrollment in a night school for immigrants. Instead, she began to attend stage plays and lectures in English at Cooper Union and at Bryant Hall.

She wrote home, "I am looking for people who are discussing life and searching for truths."

She found them. And they found her. Some were real. Some were wildly phony.

Marie resumes the story in her own words:

I'm a fat girl. In Romania I was solid. I was counted as having a pretty good figure. But when I came to New York, they said I was fat.

They said, "You know, you're too fat to climb stairs comfortably. You'll have to lose weight."

"It's a strange thing," I said. "In Europe, when you're nice and plump, it's a sign of prosperity. Being thin is a sign of poverty."

Here, I quickly discovered, it's the reverse. If you're fat it's a sign that you're poor because you have to eat a lot of cheap starches. If you're thin, it's a sign that you're 'smart,' that you're well-enough off to be able to afford dieting with special foods.

I knew I was solid and healthy, with all my 165 pounds. But I said, "What can I do?"

One of the girls I had met said, "Take a soup-spoonful of vinegar after each meal. I was like you are and I took the vinegar treatment and the fat just melted away."

I tried it and I lost weight tremendously. In fact, thirty pounds within three months. I didn't know how dangerous it was. Whenever I looked in the mirror, or in the store windows I passed walking through the streets of the East Side, I could hardly recognize myself. I was slenderized. I sent pictures home to Mother, and she was horrified. "Are you sick?" she wrote me.

But there were deeper things than being made conscious of my weight that made New York disappointing in the beginning.

It was the look of the city. It presented itself to me not as a gay city, as I had expected Paris or Vienna would be. It hit me as a hard-working city where everybody is grinding, dashing, running.

I found no relaxation in the streets. There was not much serenity in the faces of the people.

This fundamental feeling I've never changed. With its waterfront and all, what a beautiful city New York could have been to live in if they had put the factories on the outskirts, and built the city itself with a thought for living. No, all they thought of in New York was commerce, and commerce alone tends to make a dreary spectacle.

And yet, I soon discovered, New York is a place where you can live any kind of life you choose. There is room enough for every life and for every nationality.

For my first two years here, I clung to my Romanian clothes. They were colorful, they had a peasant touch about them. But I was determined to learn the language. I said to myself, "I'm here, the first thing is to make myself understood."

Within a year, I managed to accomplish it, without a single formal lesson. This is because I said to some of my new friends, who thought I should go to night school, "No, I don't want to learn non-practical words that don't interest me. I want to learn through words that interest me."

I had the phonetic help of my Romanian, which has many words from the Latin, just as many words in English come from the Latin. Basic words.

Meantime, I hunted up a man named Hugh Pentecost who used to lecture at Bryant Hall. He was a former minister and rabbi who talked about exciting subjects—"What Life Means to Me," for example, that was the title of one of his lectures. Yes, he was a radical, but the kind of radical who used beautiful words. It was good to learn from him. Justice, truth and fraternity.

If he speaks interestingly and I begin to understand him, I'll get some stimulating thoughts from him, I figured. For now, he speaks a fine English; I will get acquainted with the sounds.

From plays given in the English language—Shaw, Ibsen, Shakespeare—I also began to be familiar with the beautiful sounds of the tongue.

I was doing quite well when, in my search for worthwhile people, I met Peter Neagoe. He was a youngster from Romania who was then painting and writing poetry. He lived in a house, a sort of *pension*, kept by a Romanian woman who had with her a group of music students, writers and other young people from Romania. In later years, I was able to help Peter. He wanted to be a painter but I nagged him to stay with writing. The world gained. He wrote of his peasant childhood with a style of gripping simplicity.

Peter and the others took me into their group when I said, "I want to go where there are lectures and discussions." They took me one night to a place on Broadway. There I met an old man named Raskin, a Bessarabian who was a sort of philosopher. That is, out of his weaknesses he had created a philosophy. His idea was to go around finding women for himself. To further that weakness (or to justify it) he developed a philosophy of free love.

But he was a well-read man, including Balzac and all that. So I said to him, "Uncle"—we called him uncle—"Uncle, where can I go to hear some worthwhile lectures?"

He said, "Well, you still don't understand English altogether too well. Better go to the Jewish Center on East Broadway where you will hear lectures in Yiddish."

The next night, I went there with Peter. And there, for the first time, I saw and heard a young, blue-eyed, blonde woman whose magnetic and dynamic personality I immediately recognized.

It was Emma Goldman. Yes, she was an anarchist. The lectures were socialistic or zionistic. But what I heard in her talk was a thing about freedom for the individual from force.

I was pulled to it immediately. I said, "This is the beginning of what I want—the people she attracts, the things she says." I began to work as a volunteer usher at her meetings.

The newspapers made her out to be a she-ogre carrying bombs. The fact is, she was more like a regular *hausfrau.* She was a marvelous speaker who could make your blood run hot, but her aim was justice, not violence. We could always tell when there were police and private detectives coming in to be seated because they never really listened to her. They looked around, they wrote in little books, they encouraged heckling and fights.

What attracted me was that, there, I was finding thinking human beings.

While I was thus finding a circle, I worked so hard on lining coats that I kept five men in the factory busy handling what I put out. In hardly more than a year, I was able to prepare a little home of three rooms, kitchen and bath on St. Mark's Place. I thought of the work-laden life Mother was leading and I said, when I bring her here, I'll see that she relaxes. I went and bought a rocking chair, to make ready for that day. It gave me the kick of my life to picture her sitting there.

But first I sent for my sister, Rose. She was still only a kid of fourteen, but already she was an expert milliner. And millinery in Romania meant that you made the whole hat, you didn't just get the shape from somewhere else and decorate it. Rose could design them right from the beginning, out of wire or straw.

I went to a Romanian family I'd met in New York and explained to the man that she was very delicate, so that I couldn't afford to bring her to work in an ordinary factory.

"But she has golden hands," I told him. "She will make you two hats a day that you'll be able to sell for forty or fifty dollars and they'll be perfect."

In those days, it wasn't so easy to find such a worker. The man got interested. "I happen to be going to Romania," he said. "I'll go to your mother and meet this girl, and if she's what you say, I'll escort her back to New York."

He did. He was charmed. Rose was not the extrovert I am. She was very retiring but she had a way of attracting people so that they were called to serve her or take care of her.

And so she was with me. I guess I acted like a little mother. Each morning, before we went our separate ways to work, I stood there in the kitchen of the apartment and fixed special foods for her, for her lunch. In the evening, when she came home, there were special ways I followed for resting her and caring for her.

Little by little, I took her to the lectures and the plays. New doors opened for both of us. At night, I would sit with a coat to be lined on my lap, and we would discuss the latest thing we'd learned about Shaw or Ibsen. Almost before we knew it, we had enough money put aside to buy the two and a half steamship tickets and send for Mother, Becky and little Dave, who was seven.

Where I bought the tickets, they suggested how Mother should explain to the immigration people at Ellis Island about having left her husband behind. I wrote to her that they would ask why didn't Lupo come, and that to save embarrassment she should say he remained behind because of business affairs.

That letter didn't reach her in time. But the wisdom and diplomacy of the woman! When they asked at Ellis Island, she bit her lip and said, "I don't want my two daughters to know it, but my husband is dead." The immigration people were filled with compassion for us—why, I didn't understand until later—and the whole thing was settled.

It was evening when we got them home to the apartment. Ambition was realized, Mother was free of tyranny and toil. But early the next morning—I might have known—she thought it would be good to fix breakfast, to make Rose and me feel that Mother was here. She got up quietly, before the rest of us, and went out into the confusing strangeness of sights and sounds in the street to buy rolls.

The stoops in front of the row of buildings were all the same, so when she went out she made note of the shoemaker shop downstairs as a landmark. What she didn't know was that the truck at the curb was there to move the shoemaker away. By the time she got back, there was no more shoemaker. She was lost, she didn't know which stoop to go up.

What do you think she did? When we'd brought her the evening before, there had been a whole commotion among the neighbors as I announced that my mother had arrived. So she knew that the neighbors were aware of her presence.

She went up to a stoop. "Is Mrs. Yuster here?" she asked the woman standing there.

The woman looked at Mother and said, "Of course Mrs. Yuster is here. Sure, you live here." Mother came up to the apartment laughing joyously, her arms full of bundles.

Later I told her, "Mother, you can choose what kind of life you want to live here. You can go with people your age, and do things they do, or you can be with us. We're going to lectures, we go to the theater, we're working hard at educating ourselves. Who do you want to be with?"

She didn't hesitate. "With you!" she said. And she began to participate in everything. We took in lectures and we discussed, and she was right there in it all.

From Lupo in Romania there began to come the saddest letters. At first, he hadn't realized what was happening to him. He took for granted that other people were interested in him. But from the day Mother left, nobody invited him anywhere. They began to shy away from him. As two years went by, he realized in his loneliness what it meant to him to have the family.

"Why have I been deserted?" he wrote. "Where is my beautiful family?"

I began to watch Mother's face as she read such letters.

"Of course he has to stay where he is, because of the way he carried on toward us," she said.

I said, "But my conscience is beginning to bother me." I knew that, rationally, Mother approved. We didn't need Lupo, we didn't want him with us, he had a mean nature. But what was in Mother's heart?

I thought, "Now that I've accomplished my dream, now that I've gotten her away and showed the man the lesson that it could be done, now there comes the question of what Mother's heart is saying."

I gave her a whole questionnaire, an interrogation. I looked into her eyes. "Do you still love him?"

There was a twinkle there. And a wistfulness. "When you've lived so long with a man ... When you've had children with him ..."

"Are you still in love with him?" Again, she gave no positive answer. She didn't have to. I knew the answer. Imagine—with such a despot!

I wrote Lupo a ten-page letter. I enumerated his sins. I reminded him of his treatment of Mother, of the occasions when he cut off my braids and did other cruel things.

"These are interference with the individual," I wrote. "Such things do not go in America, where all of us are earning our own livelihood. If we have you come, will you leave the despot in you behind, in the old country?"

He vowed to change, and so we sent for him. He was 70 by then, but still erect, with a fine figure and a strong face.

The day he arrived, we surprised Mother. "We have a package from the old country for you," we said, and then we produced him. He loved to read, he loved the theater, he enjoyed gaiety. That very night, we all went together to see a performance of *King Lear*.

But it was not very long before I came home one evening and saw that Mother had been weeping. Her eyes were red. Lupo had been tormenting her about how late we girls stayed up talking and then had to get to work the next morning. I confronted him with it. "Mr. Lupo, you broke your contract. We have a separate room for you on the East Side. Pack up."

He looked at me, his face pale. "Why?"

"You made our dear mother cry. She is not to cry anymore. She is only to laugh. This is a country for laughter."

He begged for another chance. This great tyrant begged like a repentant child caught doing something wrong. We gave him his second chance, but he had done his damage. All his life, he had lived without giving love to his family.

One evening, little Dave showed around a picture of himself and Mother. He said he'd had it made that day by an old man on the street, one of those itinerant photographers.

Lupo looked at the picture. "Why didn't you call me to be in the picture?"

The boy only spoke what was in his heart. "I didn't feel like it!" he said.

It was like somebody had poured poison into Lupo's body. All the truth of his selfish life hit him like a hammer. He got up and walked into the hall and collapsed from a stroke.

He was taken to the hospital where he wanted nobody but Mother to touch him. But I saw him every day, and each day I found he was becoming a bigger and bigger man inside.

"If you die, you die a great man," I told him. He lasted three weeks.

Mother didn't think of what he had done to her and the children, she grieved only for what he had done to himself.

"He had longings," she said. "He wanted to live. He just didn't know how."

Who knows what hampered him? It's like an electrical circuit. Some wires connect, some don't.

4. STARTING UP IN GREENWICH VILLAGE

1910. Greenwich Village and New York's adjacent East Side ghetto were the centers of ferment against the economics and the morals of an overstuffed and restrictive Victorian age. Restless midwestern youth from white, Anglo-Saxon, Protestant families supped, talked, and bedded down with young disciples from the England of G.B. Shaw, William Morris and other Socialists, and with the freshly-arrived European immigrants who expected America to live up to its announced ideals.

Small halls on the East Side rocked with debate, protests and "movements," while the rest of New York and the nation watched in horror and concluded that society was going to hell. Nothing was sacred. Big business trusts, with their private-eye goon squads, were an insult to the working man and the consumer. Marriage was legalized prostitution, an affront to the dignity of womankind. Unplanned parenthood was a yoke around the necks of the poor and a blow against the sanctity of childhood. Established art was a pickled, primrose prettiness, divorced from life. Government power was an exploiter's tool to squeeze personal liberty.

In the eyes of sedate society, the stormiest and most dangerous of the petrels was Emma Goldman. And when she chose St. Mark's Place on New York's East Side, where Marie lived with her two equally well-built sisters and their mother, as the site to launch a "free" school, their involvement was predictable. They became volunteer ushers. Through the school they met for the first time many of the young painters, writers and political thinkers who came to covet their chorba and to lust after the girls' warmth. For Marie, it was the prelude to her first Village "center."

Marie:

When I say we came to it all through Emma Goldman, that isn't to say we came as anarchists. The main part of it was freedom for the individual, fulfillment for the individual. Sure, some of the anarchists in the group believed it was all right to kill or blow up things, if necessary, to avoid too much governmental power. State power. It's ironic that forty, fifty years later the people who keep hidden guns and talk against the Supreme Court would call themselves hundred-percent Americans, and they would not be the radicals, but the reactionaries.

Anyway, Emma Goldman on many subjects made great sense. She talked of votes for women and equal sex rights, against child labor and for birth control. Believe me, that was long before Margaret Sanger, although we were then careful and called it "family limitation." And in Emma's group were what were called philosophical anarchists, who were against injustice and who wouldn't hurt a fly. "There is a screen of untruth we must pierce," she said to me once.

When the Spanish thinker, Francisco Ferrer, was executed for advocating schools that would be of free character, Emma was a leader in gathering up all the educating minds, to start a free school. This was the Ferrer School, first located there on St. Mark's Place near where we were living. And how marvelous that such a school should be started right close to where Peter Stuyvesant lay buried in the churchyard. Freedom almost on top of a man who cheated Indians. The Ferrer School would be a free school in the sense that it would have the least discipline, like the idea then that the best government would be the one that governs the least. After the quarters were set up, somebody wanted to hang out a shingle saying simply, "Here is a school." Anybody could walk in, sit down, ask questions, and come again if he was interested enough, or stay away if he wasn't.

There, in the Ferrer School, Robert Henri set up an evening art class and there I worked, helping with little things to run the class for him. Ach, was Henri a man! He taught them all—Sloan, that wonderful wild man George Luks, and the others who were just making of painting an American thing, taking from the American atmosphere—that was the "Ashcan School" and Henri taught them all. John Sloan later told me he never would have become a painter if not for Henri.

Henri was a thin, tall fellow with slanty eyes. He said to me one night after the class, "Marie, what are you doing in this sketch class to make my students so individual, so different? After all, you're not an artist." He said that he, himself, was too Anglo-Saxon to create this. If so, it was one of his few defects, for he was a fantastic teacher.

I told him, "Well, I don't bother them. I let them go on expressing themselves as you tell them. To 'paint life' rather than 'think of art'. But when they are discouraged I give them an interest, and when I see they have created something exciting, I give them a big lift to go on to something even better. But when they are just playing around I tell them maybe they should go back to Oshkosh or wherever they came from." Henri laughed and pulled me close. "We have a Freud without fee," he whispered.

Visiting critics at the Ferrer art classes were Sloan and George Bellows, who was as big and hearty as the boxers he liked to paint. He and Henri both were pleased to see that one student who especially picked me out to encourage him was Niles Spencer, later one of our fine artists and glowy people, but then just a fresh, teenaged kid from Rhode Island. "The city is a cold place, it has too many walls," he said to me once. I said, "Look, Niles, do you find me a cold person?" Oh no, no, the boy said. "All right, Niles, how about I walk out with you and I stand against some of these cold walls, maybe you see that walls make lights and shadows to put perspective on human people?" He was for it, we did it, and he made a beautiful sketch that sent Henri ecstatic.

To those who asked how did I make myself feel this way, without any regular education, I gave the answer that I was lucky. I said because I never had anybody pumping knowledge into me, I had been left free to take it from nature, and from drinking in the spirit of the people I sought out, it seemed I was thus more free to be a stimulator for those around me. This was wonderfully right with the principle of the Ferrer School, which was to draw out rather than pump in. We were often reminded at the school how, when they were executing Ferrer in Spain, he had stood at the wall and said, "Shoot straight, boys." They could shoot his body but they couldn't shoot his creative spirit.

This is the spirit that held forth at our house when the students from the art class would come, at all hours, to eat and drink various kinds of coffee, and talk and argue. It was more than just the artists. We had the poets and the writers and the cartoonists and the agitators. There was Robert Minor coming around in corduroy pants and a slouch hat, looking like something out of one of his cartoons in *The Masses*, and others like Ben Reitman, Emma Goldman's wild and dangerous sweetheart, with cap pulled down low over his eyes, and Sadakichi Hartmann who looked like a long bamboo stalk and had a crazy brilliance and would shout, "I do not care who admires me as long as I admire myself."

We had moved by then to a house in the Bronx, but this made no difference, except that the new neighbors would see all these people who looked strange to them and they would worry. They said we were "different." Well, we were. You could sometimes hear for a block the arguments and the debates about violence and marriage and sex and discipline, and once one of the extreme anarchists even came to hide because the police were after him.

But to show you the marvelous link between our house and the school—the sort of link that was soon to pull me to the Village—there was brought to the Ferrer School one day, by a man who said he was the father, an inarticulate, emaciated little boy of about 12. In later years, he won international art recognition under the name of Benno, but then he was Benny Greenstein. The second or third night at the Ferrer class, he already was doing some of the best drawings there. A rat-like boy, he had a long neck, a long head, and a mouth like a whistle. He didn't even speak English so when Henri, seeing the quality of his work, wanted to tell him so, he thought the boy was Greek, and he spoke to him in Greek. But no communication.

When I noticed this, I went over and said to the boy in Yiddish, "Verstehst du?" Did he understand? Yes and no. He understood Yiddish, but not Henri speaking Greek. So I interpreted Henri's comments, that Benno was doing some very nice work. Well, he continued to come in for lessons with Henri, until one day he pulled me by the skirt, asking me to go somewhere with him. He took me out to the street to a spot a block from the school, where he showed me several pieces of remarkable sculpture. "I did these, secretly," he said, "and my father threw them out, and me too." It developed his father had him living in a dark room without windows, and now he wanted no further part of this child or his art.

So I took him home—way up to the Bronx, as people would say. I said, "Listen, boychick, from now on this is your home. Here you can sculpt, here you can draw. Sunday morning I'll invite some of the students up here, and we'll have a drawing class right here. But you've got to continue to go to school, and I must take some of your sculptures to show to Mr. Henri, because he's unaware you've been sculpting." Well, he was overjoyed. And after I'd taken some of his sculptures to Henri and Henri had kept them for a few days, he told me he had displayed Benno's sculptures to a connoisseur. Henri told him, "Look what I came across, done by Michelangelo," and the man believed him, they were so beautiful.

All the people coming to our house said, "We must take that little boy and keep him in our bosom." I washed all his things, I kept him clean, and each time I took him with me to the Ferrer school, Henri would dance around him like he was a little doll—around this insignificant little boy. But sometime later, when Henri had it all arranged for one of Benno's pieces to be exhibited at the distinguished McDowell Club on 57th Street, so the boy might be taken on by some established sculptor, the day of the exhibition came and there was no Benno, no Benno sculpture. Henri came to me, furious. "What happened to him?" he asked. I called the boy in. "Oh, I don't care," he said, looking straight at us like some little gargoyle. "I did a piece and I took it to the door of the place, but then I smashed it because it wasn't great. I must do only great things."

To round out Benno's story, I must jump ahead to when I already was established in the Village, because when I moved there I took a separate little studio for him, in what is called Clothesline Alley. He was to come get his food in my place. And as he began to grow, very fast, very thin, very long, anybody appropriate who'd come to my place I'd say, "Look at this kid's talent. Give him a commission." One day, Benno was gone, and the next thing I heard was from the police. He'd gone out to Long Island to play pirate, tried to tie up some stranger with a rope. I called Henri and Bellows: "Our great little artist is in jail." So Bellows, who as I've said was a most imposing figure, a tall, blue-eyed handsome man, he went to court to get him out. "Can you call this boy a pirate?" Bellows asked the judge. "When we were young, we were adventurous too," he said—whereupon Benno shouted, "Yes, but you didn't have the purpose I did!" and he produced a marvelous little bust he'd made of a pirate figure.

Benno was already a young man when he left me. I remember he had Dorothy, a little blonde with lots of character in her face, modeling free for him because she was mad about his work. One day Benno came grumbling to me, raging mad because she hadn't kept a modeling date. "I will be like Michelangelo, he made slaves of his models," Benno said. "I'll build a closet and keep my model locked up in there!" Later, Dorothy came to tell me why she had not showed up. "This dried up little thing tried to make love to me," she said. "He said he had to feel his subject to really feel his work." Later Benno went off to sea, and after that with $10,000 he won in competition he went to Paris, where Picasso saw his sculptures and, I'm told, fell on his knees. But Benno was convinced he should be a painter and, I understand, became calm, mellow and aloof, and called himself a Scotchman. With his nose hooked into his mouth, yet—some Scotchman. A case of fine talent in an odd shell.

This was just one strand that came out of the tapestry of our days in the Bronx that led to my times in the Village.

I shouldn't say that those first gatherings where people came to get off the edge of the ordinary happened in the Bronx because "Bronx" was and is an abused word.

Even then, the Bronx was looked upon as having a lot of dumbbells living there. Cows. They didn't think in terms of human beings living there, too.

That is why I tried to abolish the word "Bronx" in my lifetime. Another such word is "adore." I knew a woman who would say, "I just adore pastry." It took a psychologist to cure her by giving her pastry on a platter every time she said it, so that finally she could learn to save words like "adore" and "love" for real, not abused, meanings.

I try to use words that are impregnated words. So I would prefer to say it was to 200th Street, not the Bronx, that the people were drawn to make up our circle.

One of them was Will Durant. He became well known as a wonderful interpreter of the literature of philosophy but then he was the principal and, in fact, the only teacher in the children's end of the Ferrer School. To understand his beginnings is, in certain ways, to grasp a clearer understanding of the spirit of that time and the meanings of this time.

And if you look up a book Durant wrote many years ago, which he called *Transition*, and which is plainly autobiographical, you will find parts of the story as I saw it.

Will had been in Newark first, in a seminary where he was studying to be a priest. And this millionaire, Alden Freeman, who is called "Henry Alden" in the book, went to hear him lecture at the seminary on Socialism. Freeman was the son of a big mogul at Standard Oil.

When Freeman heard Will lecture, he decided this was a brilliant fellow and had no business becoming a priest when his free ideas could only be heard in other ways. He should be an educator, Freeman thought. Today, priests can be different, they can even be honest in their feelings about sex.

Anyway, Freeman brought this word to us at the Ferrer School and we invited Durant to lecture there. That fixed his future, in a sad way but also exciting, in that Durant's lecture was about the sexual nature of all religions and church steeples as phallic symbols. He even raised the possibility that Christ was a homosexual.

Maybe today, when we think more clearly and cleanly about sex, it would be acceptable, but then it was terrible. Durant had to leave the seminary. Freeman said to us, "He would be the most marvelous principal for the childrens' Ferrer School, and I am willing to pay his wage if you will accept him."

We fell for the idea, and Durant proved magnificent. He was "Bill" to the children. A short, pimply fellow but, I tell you, himself almost like a real Christ. That was the Ferrer idea of education; the children don't look to the teacher as a master, but rather the teacher learns with the children.

And one day there came to the door of the school a girl of 14 or 15 and I answered and she said, "Can I join this school?"

She was terrible looking, a gutter child, well-developed in the breasts but neglected. It was pitiful. I said, "Who are you?" and she said, "Oh, I live in the neighborhood. I hang around that laundry there, my mother and father aren't living together again. At the laundry, the men feel me up. I want to join this school."

And this little Russian-Jewish child, Ida Kaufman, eventually became Will Durant's wife, Puck. Her mother would have killed me if she had known I was, in effect, going to throw her into the arms of a *goy*, but this is how it happened.

I got up at the school board of directors meeting and said, "We must admit this girl. She is very neglected, yet she has had the wisdom to come and ask to join this school." Parents who were there objected, but I jumped up and said, "If this school doesn't mean to have a child like this, it doesn't mean anything."

So she was admitted, and I told her to go upstairs and talk to the teacher. She goes up and one of the first things she says to Durant, as she sees all the children sitting around him, is, "Will you live free love with me?"

He had understanding. He asked her, "What do you know about free love? Do you know what living with a man is?" He made a lesson of it for the day, so that not only she but all the children would understand about sex, to be taken wholeheartedly but not thoughtlessly or lightly.

And she said, "I didn't mean that. I meant that I should help you with the children and take them out together and roller-skate to school together."

Durant shared it all with the board. He made a lesson of it. Meantime, she came to me and said, "I never saw such a man. This man is a pure man. He talked to me like a person. Nobody ever talked to me like a person."

Durant told her to come back after three months. He thought she would forget it. But she didn't. She came, she helped him with the children, she was very conscientious. And soon there was love. Durant saw in her a chance to mold a wife, a Walt Whitmanish, free-spirited girl who had come to say, "Live with me."

A commotion started with her parents, but Durant wrote a most beautiful letter to the board and said what he proposed to do and that, if the board objected, he would resign and give himself to bringing up his wife. And to her he said, "With free love, I will be guilty of having given you a past by the time you're 18, so I'll marry you."

And I must say this, even though she and I had our differences in later years, a great, enduring thing came of it; he named her Puck—as in the book, he called her "Ariel"—and they remained together always.

During the time they were getting ready to be married, he discovered she had a hidden brilliance. She wrote a couple sketches about some nuns, and she also wrote an essay on Nietzsche, which she gave as a lecture at the Ferrer School and everybody was amazed. Durant set out a regular program for her—such and such to be accomplished at the age of 19, such and such at the age of 21 and so on. But she wasn't fit for the courses he tried to have her take at Columbia, where he was studying. The way for her to learn at that time, she said, was from life experience; she'd take a bicycle and ride around and have experience.

Well the experiences that woman had made into the most absolutely descriptive letters. For example, she went to Bellevue Hospital saying she wanted to be arrested. In those days she had short hair, and went around on her bicycle in sandaled bare feet and bloomers. They asked her why she wanted to be arrested and she said why, she wanted to write a book. They thought she was psychopathic, so they put her into the psycho ward where all night she was among drunks, prostitutes and God knows what.

She cried and said she wanted to call her husband. "Well, where is he?" they asked. She said, "Oh, he's at Columbia University, he studies psychology there." They thought she was hallucinating. But finally in the morning, they tried Columbia and sure enough, there was her husband. She had to promise the doctor she would wear shoes and stockings before they would let her out.

And Will Durant and his Puck were part of our circle in those days on New York's 200th Street in the Bronx.

I connect them with Leonard Abbott—Leonard Dalton Abbott, an editor of the early *Literary Digest* and head of the Freedom Association that started the Ferrer School—because if there ever was a prototype for a truly noble intellectual it was Leonard. Durant perceived this. In his book, Durant gave Leonard the name "Ronald Dalton" but there was no mistaking it when Durant wrote:

"I was jealous when I heard him speak of personal acquaintance with William Morris and Bernard Shaw, Sidney Webb and H.G. Wells.

"I was jealous, too, of his tall figure, his dark, brooding eyes, his handsome and sensitive face. He came of a well-to-do English family that had moved to America, and he showed in every gesture the evidences of a semi-aristocratic origin.

"He was an anarchist not because he wished to use violence, but because he had a horror of violence of any sort; unless he could persuade through patient reasoning he went away with his sad smile, regretful but friendly as before. To him anarchism was the absolute rejection of physical force in human affairs.

"All who knew him loved him. The women in the group gazed up at him with eyes dripping with admiration and devotion."

Well, so much for Durant on Leonard. What I can say is that I could never be serene without having been shaken up by life. Evasion doesn't do it. Only going in deep to life does it. How does nature cleanse itself? With storms. With thunder and lightning. Afterward, the landscape is serene—but only after the storm.

And Leonard could not endure such storms, he was embarrassed and tortured by the thought of them. We would sit around and Ben Reitman, who was more a vulgar than a revolutionary, would purposely heckle Leonard with rough humor and violent talk. Leonard was giving not only his words but his family money to all the causes—he did so until the end of his life.

It is true, as Durant said, that all the women loved Abbott, but who do you think most of all? My dear sister, Rose. She was a regular shirtwaist girl, tall and slender, with auburn hair. She had been keeping close company for five years with another man, but when there came Leonard Abbott—bang.

So she went one day to meet Leonard in the lobby of a hotel on Broadway to tell him once and for all how she felt. She was dressed all in gray, a gray suit. She had beautiful hands. Leonard said he would never forget how she looked.

When Rose told Leonard how she felt, he confessed that he, too, felt like this but his concern was what would become of the other man. How do you like that? Leonard decided there was a solution, he would give the other man a trip back home to Romania.

Rose walked out like she was flying. And from that day on, a book came to Rose from Leonard every morning.

She was opposed to marriage by sanction; this can be understood. We were then reading Ibsen and others, and it was almost a mystical revelation. How could you believe in marriage by the state when you heard such ideas as the woman in *A Doll's House*, and saw that such state institutions as marriage were used to deny women an equal spirit? In fact, Leonard said, he had recently written to a friend giving Rose as an example of the validity of the free union concept.

But in the end, Leonard being Leonard and Rose wanting children as much as she did, they were married. In the spring, they had a weekend in a doll's house in Westfield, New Jersey.

In the house on 200th street, they were then living downstairs, and Mother, Becky, Dave and I were living upstairs.

The first child born to Rose and Leonard, one that died soon, Leonard named Voltairine de Cleyre. This was so much like Leonard. He was honoring an idealistic anarchist of this name. He and Rose named their second child William Morris, after the great English socialist-philosopher. And when the first baby died, somebody, I forget who, wrote a little poem. It came out of the feeling by many that society was full of injustices.

Little Voltairine de Cleyre,
Kick your feeties in the air,
Not having lived longer
You'll suffer the less,
So rather than weep
Your death I will bless.

I suppose it could also be written today, but that is something for encouragement, not discouragement; it simply means life on the beautiful earth is always a question of trying to get the tender part of human nature ahead of the cruel, rigid part.

Anyway, I said I would pick out three men in our circle to mention: Leonard Abbott, Will Durant, and Damon Marchand.

I have left Marchand for the last because for me he was the only one, the only man I ever found, to know and appreciate what I felt I was born for—the spirit of adventure, of freedom, to be used deeply, not for fickle and escaping things like some mixed-up young people do today in desperation.

Arnold Damon Marchand. Danon, I called him. Not "Damon" but Danon, like in the old country. Sometimes, just "Marchand." We used last names like first. Equality. He was 13 years older than I. When I had seen him first, as a little girl in my village, with his bristling mustache and in his uniform as one of the Queen's Cavalry, on a prancing horse, I had been afraid. I was afraid of uniforms. He had gone to travel the world, accumulating languages. He learned 300 languages and dialects. Believe it.

And now he was there in New York, in our circle at the Ferrer School and at the house and working as an interpreter at Ellis Island, where the great immigration still was sweeping through. He had a desk side by side with Fiorello LaGuardia, later the Mayor of New York.

At our gatherings, Marchand would be one of the boys but very quietly, in the corner, mostly sitting and listening. He was one of those that I admired because, while he didn't take a very active part, he always showed he had intelligence and understanding. There were a few in the group who courted me (I was what you might call voluptuous) but not Marchand.

But one day, while the discussion was going on—I think it was about the needlessness of spanking children to build in them real values—Marchand turned to me quietly and said, "Let's go out for a walk." I said, "Oh, yes, I'm dying for some air." We stood outside, trying to decide where to walk.

I said enthusiastically, "Let's walk up to Central Park." This was from the school on St. Mark's Place.

He said, "Oh, wait a minute. I'm not really interested in where we are going today. I'm asking you to take a walk, hand in hand, together, through life. I've had my eye on you for a long time, even from the first time I saw you as a barefooted girl in Europe. Why not say yes? It will be a joy."

I said, "Oh! What a way of proposing! How direct. How simple. How wonderful. Those others who have been courting me, they go around and around. You have put it so simply that it appeals to me. But you have to give me a chance to consult my heart and see how it really responds. I have to match the proposal with the response."

So off we went for this marvelous little stroll. Inwardly, I suspected it would be the beginning of a walk for life. In fact, when we returned home we both felt as though we were engaged. When I made the decision finally, the others came to me one by one and said they never dreamt this would happen; didn't I know they wanted to marry me? And I said, "The difference is that he knew how to approach me, he knew how to speak what was in his heart." Marchand proved to be a tremendous lover. Each time he held me to him in bed, he called it "Yontiff!" which is Yiddish for "holiday!" So much unlike another man in our group who would always want to talk politics right at the climax.

So there it was, and my other interests were continuing.

Everybody of exciting, searching personality coming to partake of our chorba and our beef flavored with bayleaves, and our Turkish coffee, and Robert Henri saying I had some kind of psychic divination or something to help the developing talent. Only now there was Marchand, to drop something mysterious into the pot and throw up his hands and say, "Ah! That makes it."

But how long could this go on? Suddenly, one night, several of them said, "Why should we exploit your home like this?" And I said I am not being exploited, it is like good wine for me to be a functional thing for human beings. But they said, "'No, it's not fair, our coming all this way to eat your food and drink your coffee. Why don't you open a little place for us in the Village?"

And believe it or not, at the head of this was the string of bamboo, Sadakichi Hartmann, a magnificent intellect, who looked like an Oriental emperor.

"Open a place for us," he said. "Maybe even I will pay sometimes."

Marchand was against this. He loved people but not in a public way. He was happiest when we were alone. But it occurred to me that, with such a place, he could quit at Ellis Island and give more time to his remarkable ideas and writings—in osteopathy, chiropractic and manipulation of the body, in chemistry, in technology.

Also opposed were the Durants. Durant said I would make five cents back from every ten dollars spent.

Yet the Durants said they would help, even wait on tables. It was a forecast of the future, in that I never would have ordinary waiters. Marchand would go along because it was in him to recognize that my freedom should not be hampered. Some of the deep thinkers in the group said it would be a retreat from intellectuality, but Leonard Abbott saw this would not be so. David Ross said he would not only be my first regular waiter, but it was he who came up with the name for me: Romany Marie. People later knew of Ross as a golden-voiced announcer and poet on CBS, but then he was young and strictly a poet. David of the Hills, we called him.

And why not Romany Marie? All of a sudden, I came to see that I would be connecting with my mother's life, with what I had seen her do for the people at the inn in Berlad. I never made a pretense of being a gypsy. For me, Romany was a thing of the spirit.

So I decided. I did not quite realize it would be a decision for the rest of my life.

5. The First Center

The first World War had begun in Europe, but U.S. involvement still lay ahead. Marie (and, grudgingly, Marchand) became an integral part of a Greenwich Village not yet suffering from what Marie would call "the chase for empty gaiety" that was to be induced for some in the 1920s by the disillusioning after-effects of world conflict.

"Already the uptowners, and the people in out-of-the-way places like Omaha, were thinking of Villagers—I shouldn't say 'thinking,' they were eating up the idea of Villagers as degenerate radicals," Marie said.

"Well, sure there were sex orgies, sure there were mixed-up girls from the midwest having affairs and babies. But the real Villagers were being wild in a creative way at that time, they were working to create a better world, not just tear down the old one."

A "Liberal Club" that involved Leonard Abbott and such others as author Sherwood Anderson and poets Louis Untermyer and Vachel Lindsay met regularly into the small hours to debate socialism, anarchism and unionism. The club convened in a house on MacDougal Street, upstairs from a restaurant established by Polly Holladay, a self-styled anarchist from Evanston, Illinois.

"Polly's earned a rightful place in Village history but it was only a meeting place," said Teddy Ballantine. That was the time of his association with those who launched the Provincetown (Cape Cod, Mass.) Players, out of which came the Theatre Guild: George Cram (Jig) Cook, Susan Glaspell and Mary Heaton Vorse. Said Ballantine, "Romany Marie was awaited for something more—a place of polarity, a place of warmth. It was known that Marie would serve as a kind of analyst, and not always a passive one."

Ballantine was right. Once Marie got her first place established, the war years brought a wildly variegated clientele bounding up the stairs to brood, battle, sketch or just have their hands held amid the fragrance of Marie's coffee, the aroma of her soup and the warmth of her interest.

There were the red-headed poet Edna St. Vincent Millay and her troupe of male admirers, some of whom couldn't make up their minds between the sexes but all of whom Marie said were eager to burn the candle at both ends. Painter Sloan's wife, Dolly, found the atmosphere a favorite outlet for her charging socialism and an antidote for the alcoholic and suicidal tendencies that may have been the price of her wifely devotion to Sloan's career. And lean, brooding Eugene O'Neill and his anarchist buddy, Terry Carlin, came between saloon brawls to sit before Marie's fire.

The war in Europe bled on, and Woodrow Wilson posed what some saw as a moral and logical basis for America's sending the boys Over There. As this occurred, fragmentation of the old Ferrer School group over the war issue often made Marie's a howling center for acrimonious argument, but one that the authorities began to eye warily as a hotbed of dissent from the war. Marie discovered to her discomfort that keeping an open shop for minds was tougher in wartime than keeping an open home, but she flowered. She used her victuals and her assertive vitality as tools to keep the contestants from splintering each other across her wooden tables. Nowhere else in the Village, it was said, could anybody find a better distillation of the verve expressed by John Reed, the dashing young Harvard man for whom mistaken entrapments in Russia's Bolshevik revolution were still to come:

Yet we are free who live in Washington Square,
We dare to think as uptowners wouldn't dare,
Blazing our nights with arguments uproarious
What care we for dull, old world censorious
When each is sure he'll fashion something glorious?

But the whimsied as well as the warring were drawn to Marie's. While John Reed abandoned his light-opera stance of Harvard days and was joining Max Eastman, Floyd Dell, and artists Art Young, Stuart Davis and Peter Arno to rail against militarism and injustice in the leftist magazine *The Masses*, another Marie follower, lanky, bespectacled Bobby Edwards came to needle the needlers in *The Village Quill*:

They draw fat women for *The Masses*,
Denuded, big ungainly lasses—
How does that help the working classes?

Marie continues the story:

The place I took near Sheridan Square was three stories up. You got to it by climbing a winding-around iron stair. And you had to go down the winding stairs to get to an outhouse. It was picturesque.

Where I established was a long narrow room with a fireplace, and in the end of it what used to be in the olden days a bedroom without windows. So we made that into a little kitchen, and the little narrow room became the dining room, with the fireplace end to be reserved as the inner circle, for the creative people who might have to be fed free, who wouldn't need to pay the regular prices.

I had been invited to do this thing, I never had been in a business like that. So I brought our personal things and decorated it like that, and did my personal way of cooking. Ben Finkle, who was for years a columnist on the Jewish New York daily *Forwards* under the name of Marshelik, said I had a gift for creating unexpected corners for privacy, and for making the places look like some sort of Arab hangout. Arab! Ach!

My cooking was continental with emphasis on the Romanian, and the main thing was the Turkish coffee and the chorba. This was light, not thick, vegetables cooked until tender, then meat balls with finely chopped onion and other things, and at the end sour cream folded in. It sold for 35 cents a dish—warming and filling and popular. The recipe was like this:

Boil stock bones.

Meanwhile, chop up three leeks, three stalks celery, one carrot, parsley, two onions, one #2 can tomatoes.

Remove bones, add vegetables. Boil several hours.

Mix: 3/4 pound chopped meat, 1/2 cup raw rice and diced onion, forming into little balls. Place in vegetable soup and boil one hour.

Beat up two eggs with 1/2 pint sour cream. When balls and vegetables are done, stop the boiling for 10 minutes. Then fold in the eggs and cream. Add juice of 1 1/2 lemons and sprinkle fresh dill.

And all these people who had invited me to open, all the students and others came, and everybody who saw said who is this mysterious woman who just opens up and she gets people? All the people that I knew from the Ferrer School came there instead of to my home.

I called it Romany Marie Tavern, but this is the thing—call it a "tavern" like from Christopher Marlowe or Ben Johnson, or call it "café", the thing was it was not a restaurant; it was a center. Not just to give food to somebody's stomach and get profit out of it and then go home.

It's a functional thing where, when I'm through with the night's work in that little place, I'm renewed because I've had my relationship with creative forces, with the human element.

There would sit David Ross, not just waiting on tables but reading his poetry, or Max Bodenheim, or Harry Kemp the tramp poet whom all the girls ran after, even though he had a reputation for never carrying a wedding ring in his pocket.

And the idea was working. The young spirits in the Village were in their dark little rooms writing or composing or painting, and at a certain moment they'd stop in their creativity. They wanted some Turkish coffee or they wanted to say something to somebody about what they had created—so my center was there.

They would run in, and whether I would be making my chorba, my soup, or whether I was broiling a steak, they'd come over to me with terrific enthusiasm. Like I remember Edgard Varese. So handsome and dashing, with wavy hair, that he said he'd look in the mirror and wonder who that Frenchman was.

"Let me tell you where I am going in this composition, you will cook the chorba better," he said one day there. "You know what I have in mind? I'm standing on a great mountain and I'm hearing the beautiful sounds of the universe and with them are coming the sounds of the day, the sounds of the machine, of civilization."

I'd look at him to see if his mood was authentic for him—I'd smell his mood—and if it was authentic I'd say, "Good, good, don't forget to put in the bubbling of the soup pot," and he'd laugh, refreshed.

Can you imagine bringing that into my little kitchen? Could I think of profits of money, when such a greater richness was brought to me?

So I knew the idea was working.

But before I knew it, those buildings I was in—they were like twin buildings with a bridge between—there were eight other places. The Will O' The Wisp, the Aladdin Lamp, the Pirates' Den, and about five other places.

You walked into a courtyard and you saw these signs. Another one, three flights up, was the Sea Maid. That was an artist's girl who opened up a little tearoom. And the Black Bird. About nine places in all.

It came to be like Coney Island. I was sandwiched in among all those places, and this was bad because they were superficial places and I began to get a lot of sightseers who came to the other places out of curiosity. I had a lot of poets and writers and others and they were having to fight their way through these sightseers.

It gave me a worry, that my people would have it spoiled for them. It was a danger to the lingering tempo. Like Eugene O'Neill. So quiet in my place. He was then on his way. He had gone with Terry Carlin, a big, drinking, IWW Wobbly, to Provincetown where Teddy Ballantine and Jig Cook and Susan Glaspell and the others were having their summer workshop. O'Neill had a trunkful of plays, and somebody said that sounded rather alarming but then they gave a listen and—miraculous!—he had *Long Voyage Home* and *Zone* and *Bound East for Cardiff.*

And O'Neill was coming to my place in the few hours between the time the Hell Hole closed for the night and the time it opened again to serve drinks in the morning. He'd sit in front of the fire, staring in, and he would tell me, "Thank God there's a place that serves something besides food and sights to uptowners."

The Hell Hole, or the Golden Swan, was at Fourth Street and Sixth Avenue. There is where O'Neill did his drinking—my place had no drinking—and there the Hudson Dusters used to hang out. They were thieves and all that, a regular gang.

They would watch for sightseers coming out of the Village places and roll them for their money. But they had a great appreciation for O'Neill somehow. They loved him. Maybe they sensed he was also on the outs with the polite world. I told him it was not all mixed-up cruelty, but he said there was too much to be excused. One time he told me a man in the Hudson Dusters had suggested when O'Neill was without an overcoat in the winter that O'Neill should go to an uptown store and pick out an overcoat and this man would go up and steal it for him.

Anyway, this one night, quite late, my place was full of people when in walk the Hudson Dusters. Six of them. The people recognized them and cleared out. The people ran.

The strongest drink in my place was the Turkish coffee, 25 cents for a little cup, after which I would do a reading in the grounds. And the Dusters sat down and ordered a round of Turkish coffee. The waiters had gone, it was only Marchand and me. And the Dusters ordered another round, and then another round. Marchand was standing in the kitchen, I think dying with fear. We thought they were waiting to hold us up.

I held myself very calm and I smiled to them and I continued to bring out the coffee, and they had a fifth round. The leader then looked up at me and I looked him straight in the eye. I said, "You've had enough coffee now."

You know what he did? Took out money, paid me for all five rounds and they left.

You know where they went? Straight to Eugene O'Neill at the Hell Hole. He came later to tell me, and I treasure his account of it.

Straight to him and they said, "Jeez, what a woman. She knew who we were and she looked us in the eye and actually told us we had enough coffee. Meaning, get the hell out of here."

O'Neill said to the leader, "What business did you have going there?

You know they are my friends. I bet her husband was peeing in his pants with fear. I want you people to promise me never to go there again." And O'Neill said they told him, "We'll do more than that. We'll protect that woman. Jeez." And I was protected.

That drinking friend of O'Neill's, Terry Carlin: O'Neill made him the Larry Slade character in *The Iceman Cometh*, which was really set in the Hell Hole. Believe me, I should know, because one night Carlin came in asking me for thirty dollars. Thirty dollars to a big, strapping anarchist who boasts that nobody has ever caught him working! Oh, but Carlin tells me, Hutch Hapgood is good for the money, Hutch being the writer in whose Provincetown cottage the very first Provincetown Players' shows were presented. So I gave Carlin the money. Then some instinct tells me to check up with Hapgood. Hapgood shouts, "Thirty dollars? I meant for him to have three dollars." It turned out Carlin wanted to give a big party for the Hudson Dusters. So there went twenty-seven dollars. But still, as we all agreed, he was a beautiful man.

Another character O'Neill put into *Iceman*—Hugo Kalmar—he was Hippolyte Havel in real life. He was another one who came into my first place, along with more serious people. Havel was a chap who was in love with Polly Holladay. She rejected him and rejected him but finally she let him cook for her in her place; he did make a wonderful goulash. He also was a writer who didn't care to publish, so he sold a lot of his stuff to other writers so he could have money to drink. Havel was a little fellow with a black goatee, he owned only one shirt and one set of underwear but he was always sparkling clean because wherever he'd go to visit somebody he'd wash his clothes in their place. He was a friend of Bakunin, the famous Paris anarchist, and of Emma Goldman's, but although he was very gentle in a way, he was a very big pest. I had to throw him out many times.

The reason I think of him in this connection is to give a feeling of the Village at that time, because one night Floyd Dell walked in, a wonderful talent and a good friend. A tiny chap, looked like a vegetarian monk but he didn't write like one. Dell had been to an editorial meeting of *The Masses* Magazine, which he was then editing. They were having a big conflict between the writers and poets on the one side and the artists like Art Young and such on the other side, and so they were maintaining editorial voting to see what should be published.

Hippolyte Havel shouted, "Bourgeois pigs! Voting on poetry. Poetry is something for the soul, you can't vote on poetry." Dell said he argued with this, pointing out that collective editorial decisions had been made by Havel and others working on Emma Goldman's anarchist magazine, *Mother Earth*. But Havel answered, "Sure, sure, we voted—but we didn't abide by our decisions!" Dell fingered his coffee cup and said to me, shaking his head, "Such 'freedom' will one day rule out the romantic view of babies because order is required to change their diapers, and without the order of changing they will smell."

Could Dell continue to come in to muse about such things surrounded by sightseers? Could Theodore Dreiser feel comfortable coming in to lecture in my place, as he did? There was a misunderstood man in many ways. Marchand understood him; one night, in the place, Dreiser was under attack for supposedly neglecting his writing potential because he was spending so much time trying to get a particular girl to sleep with him. He had many passions, you know. Well, Marchand went to his defense. He shouted, "Here is a man for whom sex is never divorced from his creative force. If he wants a new woman it is because he glimpses a new character." He looked to Dreiser, who nodded agreement.

I worried that all this would go, that we were being invaded by all the sightseers, so I went and moved into Christopher Street, Number 20 Christopher Street. It was a little house that we paid fifty-nine dollars a month for, the entire little house. Marchand and I were living upstairs; there was a yard and there I put tables. And that is the place that first really became famous, in New York, in Chicago, in Paris. Famous among the people who had the spirit. I had to take it without a lease, because it was for sale. I took it from month to month, and I stayed there eight years.

That became the place that was painted so much. John Sloan made an etching of it. He and Dolly especially loved it. She was the salt and pepper of his life.

On the door of the previous place, I put a sign, "The caravan has moved," and gave the new address.

This was something I repeated for the next 30 or more years, through eleven different places. I didn't tell the people I was moving, I didn't advertise it ahead. I'd get everything all ready by five in the morning, and at six a truck would come and move everything to the new place where we would fix up the new dining room and we'd cook. That evening the people would come to the old address, they'd say, "Hmm, what's happened?" and they'd read, "Romany Marie's Caravan has moved to so-and-so."

Not very efficient, but what's with efficiency? Into every new place, they would say for the first two hours, "Oh, it's not the same!" but in miraculous time they'd get the same attachment and say the same things about the new place. And the reason for "The caravan has moved" was to make a continuation. Do you have a different life when you move from youth to age? From despair to joy? No, it looks different but the elements are the same, and this was my effort with the centers.

This is how it worked for the first time with Christopher Street, although it was a sad age in which to begin a bright chapter.

I say this because the country was moving into war, and it broke up friendships and attachments. Looking back, it is easy to see how ironic it was to call it a war to save the world for democracy and a war to end war. But at that time a lot of the radical artists and writers went for the war, and the pacifists and others didn't. My place roared with disagreement.

Like Anna Strunsky. You know, she was one of the three famously-beautiful Strunsky girls, daughters of Papa Albert Strunsky, the Village property-owner. Anna got one of the three wealthy Socialists in the Village. Rose Pastor Stokes got one, our own Rose got the second one with Leonard Abbott, and Anna Strunsky got William English Walling. And he turned against her over the question of the war; he favored the war.

There was a terrible hysteria, like after the second war with McCarthyism. Of course there were still the crazy things.

Like when Gertrude Drick discovered the little door at the bottom of the Washington Square arch. Gertrude was a pupil of John Sloan. She was the Golden Bird in the poem by James Oppenheim.

That one night, she and Sloan and some other old friends of mine—Betty Turner, Ellen Norton, Harrison Dowd, Marcel Duchamp—they were going around, drinking and looking for mischief, and they got the idea that things were getting so terrible, with Woodrow Wilson and the country being dragged into war, that the Village should declare independence from the rest of the country.

So what did they do? They went around and collected some bottles of champagne, and sandwiches and red balloons, Chinese lanterns and a red flag. They even got hot-water bags to sit on.

And they went through the little door and up the stairway to the top of the arch, and made a declaration of independence. Morning showed the Arch with the balloons and the red flag flying from the top. Years later, people went up and found some bottles of champagne still there.

Things like that happened—they were classical things. That Hippolyte Havel, he started going up to policemen and saying furiously, "Why don't you arrest me? I'm an anarchist. Why do you arrest all the other anarchists and you don't arrest me?"

Of course, it came so that anybody who disagreed was called an anarchist, later a slacker. And in a way, this led to the terrible experience I had in my place.

There was a young chap there one night, a redhead, who was studying psychology, and some uniformed boys came into the place. They began to discuss the war.

And this wonderful psychologist—some psychologist!—he found it in his head to say to one of the young soldiers, "I'd rather be a bum than wear your uniform"—whereupon this soldier got up and wanted to tear him to shreds.

I went to the young soldier and I said, "Look, my dear fellow, this is a place of business, it's not the front. If you want to fight, go to the front."

"But this is your country's uniform," he said. I answered, "Yes, but it's an insult to that uniform to fight in my place." So I put him out and, of course, I gave hell to the psychologist, saying, "Is this a time to talk like you did?"

Well the soldier went straight to his headquarters and reported me, that I'm harboring anarchists. How do you like that? And did I get it! They couldn't directly get at me for something like that so they framed me, saying it was an immoral place. And I had a trial. I took as a lawyer a man named Sabatino who later became a big judge but then he was a little student lawyer. I took a little lawyer because I wanted to show I'm not afraid. I defended the case but I took him for legal advice.

First thing when I came in the courtroom the man who arrested us told me on the side if I'd pay him fifty dollars he would purposely get mixed up on the stand. I said, "I promise you, you'll get mixed up without the fifty dollars." The first thing I did was to tell that to the judge.

This arresting officer had an affidavit made out that could have sent us to jail forever. Full of lies.

To show we were running a "disorderly house," he said on the walls I had drawings of nudes and that people would go over and ask about them and Marchand then would get up and explain in dirty language. How do you like that for a way to tell about sketches by Zorach and Stuart Davis and Joe Pollet?

So they put Marchand on the stand, they had his little book that he'd written on languages—*Language Is Power.* The judge said to him, "You speak many languages?"

"Yes, your honor."

"Do you ever speak profanely?"

Marchand got furious. "No! I don't know what that means." Of course, he didn't call the judge a son of a bitch, as he might have in the restaurant.

The way that affidavit was framed, one of the things the detective said was that a woman came in and sang a dirty song, "Every little bump is a nice little bump, a nice little bump for me." It went on like that, very vulgar, and the detective was supposed to have remembered the verse because about 30 minutes later, after he'd gone up to the elevated station, he'd written it down.

Ah, I thought, here's where I'm going to mix him up. I said, "This man boasts here that he has a very good memory. Your Honor, I would like my lawyer to read one line from Shakespeare—one line—and have that man repeat it. A man with such a memory!"

Well, he fell through. It was something from Hamlet. He fell through.

I had men and women of good standing there to testify to my

character. In the first row I had some Ph.D.s, all kinds of young girls from N.Y.U., one girl from Boston, a high-minded, beautiful creature, and I said, "Your Honor, before this affidavit is read, I would like to have the first row of young ladies removed to the back row, I don't like them to listen to this affidavit. It's too vile for them to hear."

The judge called for one of the Ph.D.s and asked her, does she live alone? She said, "If living with 40 other girls means living alone, yes."

He said, "What do you do?" And she said, "I've just graduated. I've just made my Ph.D. This is the first time I'm using my title as a doctor of philosophy, to testify for Romany Marie's character, and I'm proud of it."

You know, there was Lola Ridge, the poetess. In her *Broom* publication appeared some of the first works of such as Waldo Frank, Edgar Lee Masters, Amy Lowell and Conrad Aiken. She herself had written a book called *The Ghetto*. It was fierce revolutionary poetry. And that detective was such an ignoramus, he brought her book as proof I had a disorderly house, because in it she spoke about the nudity of some people because of poverty.

Well one of my witnesses got up and said, "The worst thing I ever saw happen in Romany Marie's was when Maxwell Bodenheim read his poetry."

In the end, the judge knocked his gavel and called over the detective and said, "Why did you frame these people?" Then he knocked his gavel again and said, "Not guilty." There was a terrific demonstration in the courtroom; the spectators were for us.

It was a terrible thing. Yet it had some importance in my thinking because it was a kind of bookmark on the end of one chapter, part of a curtain on one act before the next great acts of the play began.

I mean the 1920s and '30s and '40s. Not to be lumped together, but not to be given the easy definitions too many people give them.

Like the end of the first World War led to the period which some people call the Roaring Twenties, and they pick out only the flappers and the bathtub gin and all that, but overlook the real character. This was the time when many of the old Village crowd began to succeed uptown and nationally and internationally but some of them remained in the Village. And they were joined by a new crowd, of which some were degenerate, and some were pseudos seeking escape into superficial gaieties, but others were real and sound.

Sure the crazy things went on. At the fountain in Washington Square on hot summer nights, my God, they'd take off their clothes and go in swimming.

There was Doris Carlyle—a character who lived once with Oscar Wilde's Carlyle—she was an amazing person, she took off her clothes and went swimming. A policeman came and said, "Put your clothes on, I'll walk you to the station house."

She said, "You found me this way, you'll walk me this way. I won't put my clothes on." She stood there in front of the policeman, and her crowd of friends stood there with her. As he insisted that she dress, she suddenly turned and said:

"You ought to be ashamed of yourself. A nice, big, Irish fellow, probably have a wife and children at home, standing and staring at a nude woman. Shame on you!"

He walked away. He walked away! Doris the Dope, they called her. Said she made her living coughing, like Camille.

The Village was misadvertised on this, especially after the first war. What I'd say is that in the long run there were more pseudos that tried to hide themselves under great people's creation than there were degenerates. In any case, there was a great wave of writing about it in the newspapers, saying the Village had nothing but degenerates or pseudos. They didn't mention those who were sitting in their studios, creating.

I had simple people coming to my door, licking their lips and saying, "Is this the place where the free lovers are?" People from all over the country who'd read the stories. If they came into my place and observed the other kind of people, sitting in one corner to write, in another corner making designs on napkins for what they were going to do, and then they would have a talk with me, often they would change their minds.

I'd say, "There are those who've opened places especially where you can see the wild ones.

"But that isn't what my place is mainly for. My place is for those who are seriously searching, and others come who enjoy such atmosphere."

In the Christopher Street place would come Edna, the little lady poet. Edna St. Vincent Millay. She either came in very gay with her group, like Witter Bynner, Rose O'Neill who made pictures like angels, the Kewpie woman, and all that, or she'd come in alone.

She'd sit in a corner and either think or read something. Many times I'd say, "You want something?"

"Oh Marie, Marie, Marie—yes, a lot of Turkish coffee."

And then she'd turn over the cup and say, "Read it to me."

With her, I'd say something cheerful about the cup. Edna needed cheer. I'd say, "You ... this and this and this ... is going to happen to you." And the mood was changed, you see. Edna drank this in. One evening she looked at me over the cup, much troubled. "Marie, do I look like a prose writer to you?" So what does a prose writer look like? But I knew she was not making a living from her poems or from one very fine play done by the Provincetown, yet she was not happy with the money from prose she was writing for magazines—under a different name, yet. I had heard some poems were getting a good consideration at *Vanity Fair*. So I looked in the cup and I said, "I see coming up a new proof that you are loved for your poems, as much as for yourself." Two days later she got an acceptance of poems by *Vanity Fair*, and came in to embrace me and say, "Marie, you were a bridge for me over two empty days."

The way I did was not to push, not to encourage that sort of reading thing. Instead of letting myself preach to them, I suppose I tried to be a psychic reader. When I wanted to give cheer or new hope or new energy, I'd look in the cup and I'd say, "Look, there is a shadow going out of your life and a brightness coming in." It was a feeling I'd get, and often correct. All these people had writings sent out to publishers or works to galleries. They were in anxious expectation. Sometimes they'd ask, "Now where do you think I ought to send this?" Not so much with little Edna, of course, but others heard I was in contact with some publishers or newspaper persons, or at the art galleries. And immediately my mind would begin to work and I'd point out a possible way to go, and many times it hit beautifully. Of course, when I told one of them to do a thing, I would make them follow it up. A lot of people say, "Oh yes, yes, yes!" only to walk away and forget it. They are anxious when they ask, but not later. I made sure, next time they'd come in, to ask, "Did you follow up?"

That would make them ashamed. "Oh, I'm going to finish that poem now," or "Oh, I'm going to call them right now." I held them to it; time and again I held them to it.

Understand, I am not saying the serious ones were all saints.

Witter Bynner and Arthur Ficke, and Fred Leighton who was secretary to the great Russian philosopher Gurdjieff, all three would come in, they'd be drunk, they had women and they had men.

You'll see in Millay's book of letters that she was in love with Witter Bynner, perhaps she expected him to marry her. Bynner was also in love with Rose O'Neill; he was bisexed. I can say that because he didn't make any bones about it. It was a great naïveté on Edna's part to even dream anything could come of their relationship. She also was in love with Arthur Ficke—and it's true that he later married and had a very fine life.

The point is they were wild in a creative way. They inspired each other, they talked about their particular ideas and ways of writing, so if they were wild with it all, who knows? Who cares?

Naturally, I had to be a bouncer sometimes for people when they got a little off-key. Like Maxwell Bodenheim. How many times I had to throw him out.

And you know there was a period when he was mentioned right alongside Ezra Pound and Carl Sandburg and Edgar Lee Masters. A great, inside sadness made Bodenheim dissolve his genius in whiskey all through the years until the middle 1950s when he and his latest sweetheart were murdered by some bum they were flopping with.

Do you know how I would bounce the off-key ones? Naturally, self-preservation always comes in; I wouldn't put myself in a position where he could hit me or get at me. But I'd step out the door and call him out, beckon with a finger and say, "Come here."

He'd get startled and usually come out. Ah, I have him on the sidewalk now. Then I would say, "Look, do you realize you're making a fool of yourself—or don't you? How many people do you see in there acting like you are? There's only one. I would advise you—and I'm appealing to your intelligence, and you understand English—leave now.

And do it."

Invariably, "Awright, awright." The point was not to go over to a person like you're not interested in human beings and say, "Hey you, you don't belong in here, get out."

One night a man came in, very tight. I never liked people who were drunk to be in my place, so I went through the business with him and he said, "Are you throwing me out?" and I said, "Well if that's the way you want to put it."

And after he was gone, people jumped up and said, "Do you know who you just threw out? George Luks, the great painter!"

I said, "So? If he misbehaves, I don' t care who he is." The fact is, he came back, many times. He was a very amusing man and we had a lot of fun together.

The first time he returned after that drunk, he said to me, "You know, you were right. My wife throws me out too."

They did not have to be already famous, like Luks, to be admitted to what I called my inner circle. In fact, they were mostly not yet famous, or never to be famous.

Beginning with the Christopher Street place, my inner circle was composed of those who could sit at the two long tables with benches near where I had the open fireplace and the kitchen, into which you could look to see the activities there. It had to be open because this was a personal place. If some lonely or troubled person came in as they did, and asked, "Is Marie here?" they had to see that I was there. I thought in terms of living in the place. It was my atmosphere.

And in this inner circle were included those serious people, writers, artists, whatever, who could eat free if they needed to, without embarrassment. I also had a little revolving fund.

Patrons in the front dining room would say, "What do we have to do to get into that back room?" My answer was you must be creating, you must show you are somehow involved in attempting to become a greater person."

One night there came a man who was already very well-known as a doctor for curing run-down businesses. He called me over and said, "Marie, who gave you the idea of the inner circle?"

I said, "Nobody, this is what pulled me to this business. It is what holds me. It is a way of living."

He said, "You know who I am?"

I said yes.

He said, "You know what I charge for building up a business?"

I said I had heard.

Then he said, "Well, I couldn't dream up a better idea than what you have in the back there. If you ended that, you might just as well close up, because most of the people out here in front come to see how you function with that inner circle.

"Instead of your spending money to advertise it, you can put your money into the food because you have a word-of-mouth name due to it. So keep it up."

That was Manny Strauss, the big man at Macy's. Of course I could never think of advertising that phase of the place. It would have been like advertising who you are having for company at home.

6. SASHA STONE AND EUROPE

In 1920, a little souvenir folder about the Romany Marie Tavern on Christopher Street carried on its cover a paste-on courtyard photograph of Marie. She wore shiny black boots, trousers and a long, low-necked, tasseled peasant blouse. From her neck hung several strands of hip-length beads. Inside, the folder read:

> Just Suppose!
> In these sad dry days, Manhattan yawns in gigantic boredom. Broadway and its garish lights? No! Then where? Then what to do? But just suppose there was a place with a PEASANT atmosphere? A place that gave an honest glimpse of "ROMANTIC ROMANIA"? A place where coals glow on an open grate? Where, instead of jazz, come soft languid gypsy airs of the old Carpathians?
> A place where one sips Turkish coffee and fragrant drinks? A place serving a table-d'hote dinner or dishes so delicious that they tempt the jaded palate? What then? Would that amuse you? For there is such a place!
> ROMANY MARIE TAVERN

On the rear cover was a semi-cubistic drawing of a man, and the legend, "Hand printing and photo by Sasha Stone."

As things developed, Marie went alone to Europe to join Stone for awhile. Did she sleep with him? Well, this is Marie's story.

Marie:

Montparnasse in Paris and the Village in New York became like one after that first war, and also Berlin. Many in the Village were going back and forth. You could get a studio in Paris for three months for ten dollars. It became so that people sitting in a Paris café were not surprised to see friends they had last seen in my place, while many coming from Europe were arriving with a note to look me up. Matisse was one such, he came first to my place. And another who came was Sasha Stone.

It was through the chapter with Sasha Stone that I came to go to Europe for six weeks. This story I cannot tell without speaking of Marchand, because it involved so much the belief we had in each other.

There were lots of men who were in my interest but not like Marchand. Not one. Yes, there were times when I had reasons to leave him, and, knowing myself, I watched, knowing that I can't live alone, I'm a woman who must live with a man. So I watched: when and if there would be one who would sweep him out of my heart, I would be ready. Bang!

But not one, because Marchand had that faculty of knowing that I could not be tied up and bound, and that I could be trusted in my freedom. If I said to him, "I'm going away for a year," you know what he'd say?

"Watch how you cross the street. Take care of yourself."

But among the people in my places, he gave a different impression. People would leave thinking the minute they were gone, Marchand and I would be at each other's throats.

Ivan Black (you know, he was a great publicity man for the Village Vanguard and such), he remembers how one time a party of tourists came into my place from some town like Akron and they looked for a table. There were several empty ones but Marchand was sitting at the best one, eating.

In Romanian, I asked him to move, but he kept on, saying something to me under his breath. The next thing, he said, "Give them another table." And when I still said no, what does he do? He puts his plate on the floor and stretches out on the floor beside it.

"All right," he shouts, "there's your God damn table." The people from Akron run out. I am sure they thought they had seen some real Bohemians.

The thing is, when we would close up for the night, we would go to sleep in each other's arms, hands clasped. Never once can I remember did we not clasp hands. And we never had twin beds. Twin beds are for strangers, who are more interested in physical comfort than in important things.

He had a great love. When he worked on Ellis Island, and these children were coming from all over the world, always tired, always dirty and miserable, Marchand had a court around him. He would clean them up, and he had his desk full of candy. LaGuardia was the same, he always had his pockets full of candy to give away to the children. And Marchand did the same. He cleaned them and gave them candy and toys and made them happy in the new world. Children *felt* him, and so did animals.

In the place we had five cats, finally. Marchand would call them, "Hey bums!" And they would come running.

Marchand was a great person. But obscurely so because he never pushed himself. But when I began with the centers, the money business was killing for him. The joy of feeding the people and the joy of talking to them was fine, but the money business was killing, and he had no patience for phonies.

There was the night a group of Park Avenue ladies came swooping into the place. Marchand greeted them with a great bow. "What lovely girls!" Then he saw their escorts, fairies. He screwed up his face like from a lemon, and said "...and chaps as well."

But Marchand had a belief in me and when Sasha Stone came, Marchand was the one who pushed me to go to Europe.

How it happened was that Sasha was a Russian fellow who fought in the first war, for America, and when he came to New York he was apathetic. He couldn't find himself. So he isolated himself for a while. He bought a bicycle and hit the road.

This certain sculptor met him on a country road one day. Just saw him on a bicycle and talked to him and discovered what a wonderful man Stone was. Magnificent forearms. He was tall and slender, jet-black hair, looked like a Russian prince. Powerful forearms. A technician, a machinist.

The sculptor was a terrible man; he offered Sasha 50 cents a day or something, and Sasha, being apathetic and hungry for work, took it.

He went to work for the sculptor who, finally, brought Stone into my place on Christopher, and Stone got acquainted in my center.

And that summer I opened a place in the country—in Woodstock, New York. This sculptor owned a house there and I rented it from him and opened a summer place. People called it the Village with mountains.

First month, this Sasha Stone presented himself there.

I said, "What are you doing here?"

"I came out to see you. Give me a job, any kind of job. I am leaving that sculptor, he is a despot and a terrible man. He's paying me fifty cents a day; when he gives an exhibition he doesn't even mention my name for the work I did for him."

"But my dear man, I have no job for you," I said. "The only job I have here is to carry out the slops."

"I'll do it," he said. "You're the kind of woman that no matter what one does for you is not lowering."

Well, my staff there was composed of artists. Mark Tobey was one of them. Mark later said the summer he worked there was the freest school he ever had. To earn his keep, Mark had the job of washing and polishing the glasses because Marchand said Tobey made them sparkle the best. Another was Benny Greenspan. Instead of ordinary working people, I had those young artists.

Certain hours they would paint and at certain other arranged times they would do the work. Those were the most marvelous summers. The relationship there was out of this world. The one stipulation I had was that whatever they were painting, they would bring to stimulate me.

And here's a laugh. The people around there, the Woodstock natives, they first thought I was a wicked person and their kids thought I was a gypsy who ate children. I had to make some local friends and get them to sit on the porch, so the other people would know I was not a big threat.

And Marchand meanwhile carried on in the little place in town. Whatever was needed in Woodstock—paints, canvases, provisions—he collected and sent. Weekends he would catch the milkwagon at four o'clock in the morning and come out there to see us.

Well, this Sasha said, "You have artists working with you. I'm an artist too."

"You are? I know you're a wonderful technician with iron."

"No," he said, "I'm really an artist. You'll see." So I took him, and he did show he could do some wonderful things. Later that summer the sculptor and his family came out and he told me, "You'll be sorry you took this Sasha Stone on because once you have him, you'll never be able to be without him, he's so capable."

Well, toward summer's end, I asked Sasha, "What are you going to do in the fall?"

"I'll tell you what I'd like to do," he said.

"I'd like to take some little place in the Village and decorate it in a Russian 'Isbah' way"—Isbah means 'inn'—"and show it as a model so that I can get orders for more work."

It came into my head, with my having no lease on the Christopher Street place, that if I give Stone the money to find a place and fix it up, I'll have a center prepared in case the caravan suddenly has to move from Christopher Street. In the meantime I'll have two places and he'll run the one he prepares. "I'll do everything with my own hands," he said. "I'll build a Russian oven with an extension from it on which people can sit, and there will be a lot of brass samovars. People will be warm and inside the fire will glow."

In those days it could be done for $1,500. He went ahead to New York, rented a coal cellar and cleaned it out, painted wonderful friezes and all kinds of other decorations. He made that oven like a piece of art, like a piece of sculpture.

And my dears, the people flocked to it. I got a colored girl to help him, there were short orders and drinks, and since the neighborhood where he had the cellar had a curfew—on Fourth Street corner of Sixth Avenue—they closed at one o'clock and then everybody came over to my Christopher Street place, which had no hours. I would go over to the Isbah and be hostess for an hour or so each night.

People loved it. He was very tall and handsome, I bought him Russian smocks, different colors, and it was something to see him. While people came in, he painted these friezes, showing Russian scenes of all kinds.

But after three months he decided he's too much of an artist to run the place. One night I came in there, I found some drunken girl standing around, waiting on tables, and he wasn't there. Next morning he appeared, I said to him, "Sasha! That's no way to do!"

"What can I do?" he said. "I'm an artist. I thought by fixing up this place people would give me commissions to do art work, but instead I'm tied up running the place and I can't do it."

I said, "All right then, if you can't run it, find somebody and sell it." Well, he found two English girls, they bought it, and guess what? He moved in on me.

Well he and Marchand were like two boys. Marchand was teaching him chiropractics, and I had them both on my hands. Finally I said one day, "Sasha! You know where you belong?"

"Where?"

"In Europe!" I said.

Well, there's one thing I haven't mentioned. He fell in love with me. Anyway, he thought he was in love with me. When he saw my relationship with Marchand, claimed he never saw anything like it, he got it into his head that he'll never find another woman like me.

I made believe I didn't hear him. In the room where he was living there in our little house, he was doing the most versatile things. Photography, printing, sculpture—and then in the evening he would want to be downstairs in the place with me.

That was just the time Marchand began to take chiropractics seriously and he told me, "Let's have Sasha stay permanently. I'll have a chance to finish my chiropractic studies and open an office uptown, and Sasha will work with you. What's wrong with that?"

He didn't dream what was going on. This man Sasha had made up his mind he'll never leave me. He was kind of pale, with big black eyes, and when I tried laughing things off and telling him to go get himself a nice girl and get married, he got paler. Finally, one morning, he told me he had dreamed that Marchand died and I married him.

"Sasha, you're going to Europe! That's where you belong. In Europe there are millions of women like me, you think that in America I'm a rarity but in Europe you'll find millions."

When I found that he had no money, I said, "I'll buy your passage!" and I went to Marchand and said, "Let's send him off as fast as possible."

So we packed him up, and off he went to Paris. But after six weeks a friend of mine sailed back to America from there, and with her brought a letter to me from Sasha:

If I don't come to Europe to help him get started there, he's going to commit suicide.

Well, that's the Russians for you. They're for gloom and glory.

So Marchand looked at me and said, "Why don't you go? Do you want to have that on your conscience? It's summer. There won't be too much business. I'll take care of things."

I said, "Are you crazy?"

Well, Marchand kept after me. "I'll get your passport. I'll get you packed. You've never been in Europe as an adult, you haven't had a vacation in so long, the cost of living is almost nothing..." And, my God, I went!

Marchand came to the ship to see me off, and sat on deck with me for a little while, and during the trip I hardly got up from that chair where he sat. And everyday I wrote him a love letter. But something told me inside that either somebody's going to talk to him, or, in some other way, there will be a suspicion created.

So before I went off I said to him, "Listen. Remember what there is between us two that nothing in the world can touch. Remember this. There are a lot of envious people—a lot of mean people who may try to put things in your ear."

Anyway, when I arrived at Cherbourg, there on the dock was Sasha, pale, with a little bouquet of red flowers, and I said, "What are you doing here?"

"Why, after you sailed, Marchand sent me the money to come out here. He didn't want you to go alone from Cherbourg to Paris."

I said, "Look, Sasha, I don't quite know how I got here, leaving Marchand and the place, but I came urged by Marchand. And the fastest and clearest way you have to tell me what I can do for you is what I'd like, so I can take the next boat back."

He chided me. "Why do you have to tell me that? Don't I know that? Can't you give me at least a few hours of peace?"

Well, he had prepared for me in Paris a little roomette in a little hotel, next door to Edna St. Vincent Millay. And I had a wonderful time with her there. You know, Floyd Dell said she was partly a nun, partly a chorus girl, partly a Botticelli Venus.

On the boat, my dearest going-away present had been a little basket with earth in which bachelor buttons were growing—it came from a poor boy, a painter who had no money—and I had the basket there in the hotel, and every morning Edna put on a little bachelor button.

Well, I said to Sasha, I'm in Paris, I'm not going through without seeing things. I want to take ten days to see the exhibitions, the various sights, and during this time we'll discuss nothing. We'll meet in the morning, have breakfast, go around. So—he was happy.

I took him to Brancusi to show him what this man Sasha had been doing. Brancusi, you know, was a jolly, round little man, he had played the guitar in my place, was later recognized as a great sculptor.

When I arrived he was up on a scaffold and he talked to me from there. I said, "When you are finished, let's go to a café for dinner."

Brancusi said, "I no longer go to cafés. Paris is like one of our Romanian dances, a great dancing ring. You have something to say, you join in the ring. You have nothing to create or you are just waiting, you go to the cafés."

I asked, "What do you eat?"

"When we're through here I'll show you," he said. Presently, he finished, washed up, took off his overalls and took me up and across a little balcony that opened into his kitchen. He opened the stove and I was astounded. There was a beautiful, large duck. Before I knew it, he had a tableful of beautiful, cooked food.

"Early in the morning I go to the butcher's, I have fun with the women there. That's my recreation," Brancusi said. "I put the meat in the oven with herbs, set it at the right heat and it cooks itself.

"I haven't decided yet whether I'm a better cook or a better sculptor."

He began to talk about his work and gave me quite a story. How, after 35 years of doing only classical Greek-style sculpture, he went to the seacoast where he had been a boy, communed with himself and with nature for a whole year, and suddenly was able to begin involving himself subjectively with the forms of nature, rocks, mountains, ocean, and re-form them from within himself. Now he was in seventh heaven.

Anyway, Sasha. He was doing the most beautiful cylindrical work, so Brancusi (who spoke to me in Romanian) said, "So what, so what? He's an artist, he's got to work. Get a studio and work."

But when I translated this to Sasha, he answered, "Yes, but you told me I'm going to see women like you! There's nothing here but a lot of English prostitutes sitting around the cafés. I haven't met one woman like you. Look, Marchand speaks languages. Why isn't it time for him to come back to Europe and we could all have a café here?"

I said, "None of that. Now where do you want to go? What do you want to do?"

"Well, I don't want to stay in Paris," he said. "It's full of English prostitutes."

It occurred to me that with the influx that was occurring in those days from Russia to Berlin, he might have some contact there in Berlin. I was dying to find someone that he knew to pin him on.

Thank God he said yes, he had a cousin there who had gone to technical school with him.

"All right," I said, "I'll take you to Berlin. From there I go to Hamburg and take a boat home."

Again Sasha was happy. That was 12 hours from Paris to Berlin. For twelve hours he was happy.

Got to Berlin and it was something. The greatest dancers and musicians flocking to Berlin and giving everything away for the price of a dinner. First class things for almost nothing. For five dollars a week, and you could hardly spend that, I recall I walked down the street, I saw people from the Village and I treated them, I still couldn't spend ten dollars.

Well, we looked up Sasha's cousin and he turned out to be a wonderful young man doing scenic work for a theatre called the "Blaufogel." Bluebird.

When I had him look at Sasha's work he said, "My God, I'll take you right to the director." We all went, and the director was crazy about those things and hired him. It was my turn to say Thank God.

So we went out on a spree, drinking vodka and then we went to Hamburg.

But all this time I was receiving cables and letters from Marchand, and they were full of venom people had been spilling at him: Do you expect Marie to come back? She and Sasha are in love, didn't you know that?

Marchand had decided not only that I was in love but that I had deceived him, and he was in shock because he didn't believe I would do this to him. He had taken all the clothes that I left at home, put them on his arm, stood outside and called everybody to hear him say, "Look, this is all she's left me."

The cables were saying "I'm shocked" or "Take the next boat back," things like that. And the mail, my God every time I went to American Express I got this big package of mail.

Sasha said, "I feel like going to New York and killing him."

I said, "Why?"

He said, "Because I don't know of another woman in the world who deserves more to have all the men in the world without being accused. Look how you are with me."

"Ah yes, I know," I said. "That I'm not doing it is my business, but he's entitled to fifty percent of a situation and that he believes I am doing it is his business and it's logic. When a woman scoots overseas to help a man, why shouldn't he believe I'm doing what they say?

"I'm not blaming you. I'm a grown woman, I did it. And he pushed me to it. But that's how emotions are."

I found out later that the very friend who had brought me Sasha's letter had listened and believed everything Sasha had said about his love for me and how I was going to join him; she had put this into Marchand's ear.

Well, when I got aboard the ship at Hamburg, this one—this Sasha—he made a megaphone out of some paper and he shouted to me from the deck, "A great beautiful thing is going out of my life. I don't see why I should go on living."

But I sailed regardless, and as we came into the New York harbor, look! Marchand, who was well known in the steamship business, had gotten himself aboard the little pilot boat and there he stood: a big panama hat, a light suit, and he stood there with a paper covering his face, not looking at me.

With him was my mother. Before I knew it, the purser comes over and gives me a bouquet of flowers. Marchand sent a bouquet of flowers, but he wouldn't look at me to greet me.

When I went ashore and greeted him, he said, "Well, take a taxi and go home with Mother because you have no more place. I sold it. When I heard about you, I sold the place."

I said, "Ahhh, you couldn't do that without my signing it." Marchand ran off, so I got a cab and told the driver to go to Christopher Street, naturally.

When I reached there, my dear, I found the place was like a grave. Nothing was going. Then I heard a commotion.

Upstairs was Marchand, sitting on the floor, wrestling to fit an eleven by thirteen inch painting into an eight by ten inch frame. He was yelling. From outside the noise attracted Ben Finkle, the *Forwards* columnist, and Glenway Wescott who lived across the street. You know, the novelist.

"What shall I do?" I asked. "He's gone mad."

Finkle, who was a clever fellow, took a good look and said in a loud voice, "There's only one thing to do. Call the ambulance and have him committed to Bellevue."

Well Marchand stopped, glared up at Finkle, and said, "Next time, mind your own business, you son of a bitch."

Well, that's Marchand. The fact is, it still took me about a year-and-a-half to bring him around.

As for Sasha, he's dead now, died during the Nazi upheaval in Germany. But first he became great. Photographic inventions, reproduced all the arts. Made a great name internationally and some years later married a Belgian beauty. I had to write him and say bless you, go ahead, because even then his fiancée said Sasha would avoid the marriage if I wanted him to come to America.

Marchand and I were together until he died in 1949. And when that happened, he was like a saint. He wagged a finger at me for my tears.

"You're still my woman," he said.

Of course, Marchand had been terrifically magnetic to women, you understand. There was an episode that way. But that's another story.

7. THE LURE OF THE VILLAGE

Marie's return from abroad was duly noted in *The Village Quill,* a publication with insouciant brightness that was sadly unmatched by the size of its tiny circulation:

"Romany Marie is back from Paris. She says former publisher Arthur Moss is still trying to resemble Francois Villon or Doug Fairbanks in a cape." It was only a short time before the sale of the old house at Marie's beloved Christopher Street location forced her to move the caravan across the street, to Waverly Place. An ad in the *Quill* Christmas issue of 1923 bore a drawing of Marie with her hands on her hips, and the message:

"Romany Marie Tavern. Romanian home cooking *a la carte.* Turkish coffee a specialty. 170 1/2 Waverly Place, corner Christopher. New place, upstairs, with two fireplaces. More space, more air, but the same atmosphere. Marchand will speak to you in all languages."

A new place. Free ideas about sex, marriage, religion and race were now less-exclusively Village property and so those in the Village who needed to feel ahead of the game were hard put. It was in the *Quill,* edited by Marie's friend, Bobby Edwards, that there appeared in 1924 the cartoon in which a girl was telling a boy, "It's no use thinking so hard. The only unconventional thing left for us to do is get married."

Along the Village-Paris axis which Marie had just traversed, war-shaken writers and painters were dissecting and laying to rest the remnants of an American way of small-town life.

To many of the young, the enemy seemed an inhibiting dullness, and to flee it and Main Street the young from wealthy and middle-class families were flocking in ever greater numbers to New York's Village. "The lure was the Scott Fitzgerald types who didn't give a damn about social protest," recalled Teddy Ballantine. "Submerged were the Village's IWW Wobblies and the anarchists. It was now more a revolt against old manners. Down with old authority, up with the instincts of youth."

But was it a "lost generation" in a cockeyed world, shorn of all faith in the nation and the species, and seeking only to lose itself in bed-hopping and bathtub gin? "Not so for the real Village crowd," said Ballantine. "There was no money there for champagne or Sand's Point oysters. Sure it was wild, we had fun. But there was a great piety in our looseness and something Biblical in the simplicity of Village life."

As Archibald MacLeish was to note years later, "It was the avant-garde—composed in those years not, as ordinarily, of the frustrated and the defeated but precisely of the principal figures of the time."

For Romany Marie, it was a second wave of service. "There wasn't anyone who wrote or dabbled, who painted or dabbled, who didn't go to Marie's during that period," said the daily *Forwards* columnist Ben Finkle. "There were experiments in all sorts of verse forms, such as Haiku, thousands of which were written on Marie's napkins.

"In Village terms I was a substantial man. I had a job at twenty-five a week. So I was always saddled with all sorts of boarders. Marie would say, 'Look—this poor fellow—take him in.' And when he leaves me, often as not, my overcoat or my typewriter go with him."

Perhaps it was a versifier at Marie's who put her into his poetic pantheon along with Edna St. Vincent Millay, actress Helen Westley and illustrator Clara Tice:

Of actresses I like the
Bestly
I hand it to our Helen Westley,
Of artists whom I think are nice
I hand it to Miss Clara Tice,
For food providers, seems to me
I favor Romany Marie,
But poetesses never may
Be likened to our Miss Millay.

One Henry John Gibbons was really carried away:

I know a place, a tiny space
Where Romany Marie is host
And there her face with elfin grace
Smiles forth a welcome surely most
Naive. We trace from gypsy lace
Her personality. With toast
And ale a base for talk, we chase
Opinions 'round the board, and boast
With merry race of words our case
Of trouble with the world. One ghost
When laid a vase pours out the ace
To start another hand and roast
With hefty mace that sets the pace
For more philosophy to coast.
A little space, a gracious place
When Romany Marie is host.

Marie continues:

During the whole confusion of an influx of new people from all over, we saw all sorts of superfluous and overwhelming practices in the Village which did not belong to the Reason of the Village.

We treated them as such. When people came into the place who showed they wanted only to bluff their way, bluff their sculptures, bluff their poems, they were treated as human beings but they were made to feel they don't belong. The same thing with the tourists. As the newspaper talk and the feature stories told about how all the crowd of new youngsters were coming to a free-loving place, my God how the tourists flocked.

Once I told a party of them, "If you are looking to take part in wild, bootleg drinking and degenerate sex practices, if you're looking for the long-haired men and the short-haired girls, this is not the place, you will find your opportunities up on Park Avenue." Later, one of my uptown friends came in, shaking with amusement. He said, "Marie, how dare you unveil us?"

I'm not saying there weren't plenty of places that were being opened in the Village to make a profit out of attracting sightseers to look at those who had fallen by the wayside. "See that girl over there, she came here from Oshkosh or Hodge Podge and now look at her. She bums around, sleeps around, if you stay long enough maybe she'll take off all her clothes."

What I'm saying again is that there was a difference between that kind of place and mine. In the long run, the Village was misadvertised, there were more pseudos that tried to hide themselves under great people's creativity than there were real degenerates that the newspapers had such a hysteria of writing about.

The youngsters who were rushing in, the thing about them is that although they were coming from all parts of the country, expecting to be like Edna Millay if she was like her poems, they all had the same story to tell.

When they came in, I wanted to find out whether they'd run away from responsibility, whether they'd run away from too much money and a spoiling love, or whether they'd run away through a necessity to find their real expression for creative work.

Invariably I found they had run away because of the monotony of restriction, of repression. Invariably they would say, "My father is doing the same things that his father did, and society is accepting him and saying what wonderful people they are, and nobody at home sees the possibility that I might have ideas that are fresher and better and more honest."

If I found that those who were on the loose in the Village wanted the freedom only to become pseudos, I advised them to go back home, and a lot of them did. I think I did it very sensibly, I didn't say, "Go back home, you're doomed." I said, "This is no place for you, it will only encourage your weaknesses and you'll become lost. So go home and search for that little freedom you really want right there, because maybe now you will find that your parents will benefit from it, your return will help them relieve the monotony of their lives."

If they would tell me how much they liked us who were Villagers, I would explain that they were simply finding the freedom in us that they hadn't found in their mothers and fathers. So go home, I said, and tell your mother that; maybe she will be a little worried and change. I said there is such a thing as children educating their parents, without throwing into the ashcan everything that parents have to offer.

All right, so then there were the youngsters who came because they were really burning with something to say, or compose, or dance, and needed the freedom and the atmosphere of the Village to develop it. They left perfectly conventional homes to come to the place where they'd read they could be unconventional. And some of them would fly off the handle, like the girls who felt they had to try everything before they could really act or write.

Them I always told that life does not mean you have to be one-sided. If sex comes into it, and drinking comes into it, you have to do these things out of your whole being. A girl could paint or write beautifully and still remain what you call pure, it depends on her nature. True of men, too.

Often, I can size up a person, from which part of their nature they're going to create. Some kids, if their sex life is upset, everything is upset. These are the ones I called psychopaths, because a creative person, if they really have the creative urge, they're supposed to create like they eat and sleep—out of their whole self, not just out of their sex life.

Sure I had those who were writing or painting because it was a way to sublimate sex urges that they wanted to cover up, wanted to escape. It turned out to be that kind of art and sometimes it was good. But sometimes very bad, because what some of them should have done was have an affair, instead of painting a picture.

The thing is, in the fantastically mixed atmosphere we had, even the misfits and the lonely could get direction because there was nothing mushy or posy about the atmosphere. Can you imagine in the same night, among the guests, Dreiser and Durant and John Cowper Pewys, not like celebrities but being themselves? My long-time friend, Vilhjalmur Stefansson, compared it to the Columbia University Library. There, he said, people added volumes to their knowledge; at my place they added friends.

There was Bob Chanler—Robert Winthrop Chanler—he belonged

to the Astor-Vanderbilt group, a society man who broke away from his background. Used to be sheriff of Duchess County, New York, with the journalist Richard Harding Davis as his deputy. They wore chamois shirts, buffalo bill chaps and 10-gallon hats. Chanler painted screens for the 400 that were out of this world, but then he broke away and began to paint real people.

He had fallen in love with the opera singer Lena Cavalieri, and overnight almost, after he had married her, she left him. And maybe you've heard of the saying they started about him: Who's looney now? He was almost out of his head for the loss of her and so one day he got into the bathtub, and on a little phonograph he was playing one of her records and he began to cut his wrist when in walked his brother who had been under treatment for the mentals and the brother took one look and said, "Who's looney now?"

He lost his identity for a while, carried on terrible. So when he met me, he said I reminded him of Lena Cavalieri, and we had a wonderful time with him, Marchand and I, because he was a highly intellectual man.

He would come into the place and sit for hours, talking to me late at night. Finally he decided to paint a portrait of me. I began going to his studio—he had a tremendous studio—to pose—I had to go up on a platform and he would throw a brilliant light on me. One day he made some home brew—it was Prohibition, of course—and I had to drink with him, this home brew. I got up there to pose, under those hot lights, and I fainted, because I'm not a drinker.

Chanler had a lot of people around him—noisy people—he supported a lot of people, used to entertain the whole world there, in his very beautiful home in Gramercy Park. I used to say to him, "Bob, how do you do it?"

"Why," he said, "they're my performers. Look how quiet I am in your place. With them, I have to have noise." In my place, the youngsters could draw from the best side of him.

He had musicales. Everybody in the world of the arts. String quartets, singers, Isadora Duncan, all the entertainers that used to give recitals in Carnegie Hall. He had a place in Woodstock, too, so of course that helped make my place during the summers I had it there, because every weekend he would bring out a big crowd to fill it up, and this huge man—he was tremendous—used to help me wait on tables.

Finally he went to London and there he drank absinthe for weeks. The doctors said if he takes another drink he'll die. They brought him back on a stretcher, and a group of us went down to the boat to meet him. I brought him a rose and put it on his chest.

He looked up at me—I'll never forget those eyes—he looked at me and he said, "Marie, Marie! Is this how the world looks when one is sober? What a bore! What a bore!" For almost the first time in his life, he was sober. When he dies, he told all of us, the family would take his body to the cemetery but we shouldn't go, we should have a big party in his home in Gramercy Park while they're burying him. This was done.

Well, so much for Bob Chanler, because speaking of him and that period calls to mind Isadora Duncan, and there was a lesson for youngsters, because she didn't earn an income, she *lived* an income. She came into the place and immediately she and I clicked. She was preparing to give dance recitals in Carnegie Hall, and she had gone to the wealthy 400 for financial support to give the recitals. To me, she said, "I'm going to send you a bunch of tickets for those young people in the Village to come and see me dance."

I gathered together a whole bunch and imagine, when she appeared on the stage, she looked right past the jeweled people who were sitting in the boxes, past them toward us who were sitting with the free tickets in the gallery, and she said, "I dance for you, not for them." We thought it was greatness, not ingratitude, such audacity to say it was the young and the creative, not the rich, who inspired her.

But her greatness was of the kind she could only create herself. Except in theory, nobody could perpetuate it. She touched all the artists, there was no great painter that didn't do Isadora Duncan to death, but she couldn't pass on her dancing. Perhaps that is why she said "I go to glory" when she went a few years later on that auto ride, where her scarf caught and she was strangled.

The thing is, Isadora didn't lose her feeling of oneness with the Village spirit as success came, no matter how far across the world she went. Some did lose it, but many didn't.

It was a healthy thing, this success during the twenties, because it meant that Villagers were bringing the whole country a new soul, a new meaning, new arts. But it worried somebody like Bobby Edwards because he feared the Village itself was being sucked dry of its main juices. He was the one who put it so cleverly, "Eternal Villageance is the price of liberty."

I have a clipping from the *Quill* where Bobby put down his uneasiness, loaded with the names of our crowd who were being applauded outside the Village:

"In the Village no one, however great, can be distinguished above his Olympian fellows, nor is he embarrassed by not getting any deference from them.

"Floyd Dell, with white face and longish hair, hanging on the words of Edna—the great poetess herself chattering titterishly, very much as any flapper—and the complacent Villagers unconscious of these divine presences. We have seen the gloom of Theodore Dreiser fail to depress a party of oblivious demigods. We have heard them advise Nina Wilcox Putnam not to try to write.

"We have seen Gene O'Neill mildly remonstrating with the Provincetown Players and them treating him much as a person of their own calibre. Achmed Abdullah has been frequently confused with a dealer in Syrian eggetti d'arte. Nobody cheers Walter Tittle about his drypoint etchings, nor does the traffic stop for Willy Pogany. Nor do our Villagers regard Harry Kemp with any greater reverence than as the man who goes without a hat.

"The genius of Max Bodenheim is also partially and delicately obfuscated by the fumes of his careless but desperately necessary tobacco pipe. As for Red Lewis, he is never cognated with that Sinclair Lewis who wrote a book called *Hobohemia* that we never read. Concerning Lucien Cary and William Zorach, Villagers only know that they go to Provincetown during the summer.

"But, let anyone from here escape out into the world, as the above listed have edged out, he is feasted, feted and salaamed at. Even the ponderous Hendrik Van Loon—positively the worst fiddler in the Cosmos—is lionized in the middle west.

"The stupidity of the general public being discernible from what they read in the successful magazines, even the humblest Villager must

Romany Marie's 50 years in New York's Greenwich Village often saw her described by later-famous disciples as a kind of "earth mother." In her eleven different "centers" over which she presided, she routinely insisted that people be evaluated by their "many shadows."

As a young immigrant in the early 1900s, Marie learned English by attending lectures and plays and serving as an usher at Emma Goldman's radical meetings.

Marie and her husband of 35 years, Arnold Damon Marchand whom Marie called "Damon" in old-world fashion.

Beginning in the 1920s, Marie shifted her bistro hospitality each summer from Greenwich Village to Woodstock, New York, in the Catskills—"the Village with mountains." Here she is seen in her typical gypsy garb with her sister, Rose Yuster Abbott, and Rose's first child, named after the English designer-philosopher, William Morris Abbott.

A photo-portrait of Marie, one of several presented to her by George Platt Lynes, a fashion and portrait photographer widely known for his homoerotic dance images and male nudes. Lynes was a Marie regular in the 1930s. (*Photo courtesy of Lynes estate*)

With love to our great patron
Romany Mary Anisoara Stan
19 Sept 1936 San Francisco Calf.

A gypsy troupe which made its way from New York to San Francisco pays homage to its "great patron," Romany Marie.

(*Right*) "Dr." Marchand, seen here around 1920, was a linguist, chiropractor, inventor and all-around character.

(*Below*) This was a short-lived Russian tavern which Marie set up for a wandering sculptor-photographer, Sasha Stone, with whom she toured Europe.

Romany Marie Tavern

Open from 2 P.M. to 3 A.M.

Impromptu
Entertainment by
Prominent Artists
Dancing

Blue Plate Dinner
Table d'Hote Dinner
and A La Carte
After Theatre Supper
Afternoon Tea

42 WEST 8th STREET

NEW YORK CITY

(In the famous Della Robbia Room)

A Center For All Arts and Artists

Reading of turkish coffee cup and palms free - an amusement

The line, "A center for all arts and artists," stressed Romany Marie's insistence in this poster, circa 1930-35, that, while she had to cater some to Village tourists, her main goal continued to be maintaining a refuge for thinking, striving creators. While she always said she had inherited from her mother the reading of fortunes in coffee grounds and palms, terming it an "amusement" was a legal evasion.

```
        SPESHL these evening
        ---------------------

SOOPS:-  Tchorbah ,peasant soop
         Green splt soop

Choys
of
MEETZ:-  Boylt Beeph wit been's & hors radish
         Stuft peprs
         Stuft cabage

BROYLT:-
         BROYLT Chickn ( spring )
         Sir Loyn of Beef steyk
         LEM Chops

VEJETEYBLS :-
              Lone Guy Land Greens

SALADZ:-  Greens in cease on

DEZERTZ:  Qompot of fresh fruut

          Phroot qop

          Fresh peaches

DRINX:    Tee hut or qold

          Qaughee : Bleck, white, or toorkish


----- - - - - - - - - - - - - - - - - - -


        Andz analized - also vocational guy danc
```

In this 1920 John Sloan etching of Marie's second place on the Village's Christopher Street, Sloan put himself and his wife, Dolly, at a corner table.

Like her mother before her, Marie always smoked, and always wore heavy, exotic jewelry to evoke her romany persona.

Marie's husband Damon made a specialty of composing her menus in puzzling phonetics such as "vejeteybls."

This atypically roomy and well-lit location at 62 Washington Square South served Marie hardly more than a year in 1928 because of disagreements in her brief partnership with Puck (Ariel) Durant, co-author with her husband, Will, of globally popular philosophy writings.

Marie fought trappings such as tablecloths, fretting, as one regular said, that this might get her likened to a tea-room operator, which would be "like accusing her of street walking." Her husband, in foreground conversation, dispatched any such tearoom thoughts, sometimes smashing dishes if asked to make room for a patron.

Marie habitués Leonard Dalton Abbott (*above*), friend of G.B. Shaw and H.G. Wells, and painter Joseph Stella (*left*).

Edgar Varese, a pioneer atonal composer, said "Marie charged our batteries while she challenged the weak... right away she had something on you—like a loving animal."

Marie disciple, folk singer and actor Burl Ives performed in 1942 for Marie, publicist Ivan Black, and actor Zero Mostel.

This portrait of Marie by Chuck Adams occasioned her usual bemused comment that as a young woman she was "voluptuous." Of the 26 or more painters and sculptors who did her, each one got some of her, she said, but nobody caught her all. Stuart Davis said too few fellow artists captured the illusion of her being a tall woman, despite her being just over five feet tall.

This quasi-American Gothic view of Marie (*left*) was by Oronzo Gasparo in 1950. Like many other artists, Gasparo worked as a waiter for Marie until his paintings won recognition.

The celebrated John Sloan of the "Ashcan" school of American painting did this portrait of Romany Marie in 1920. (*Collection of the Whitney Museum of American Art, gift of Gertrude Vanderbilt Whitney.*)

Photos of Marie after she closed her last place to care for her sick husband, and especially after his death, seemed to show a softer Village "earth mother." But she retained her gypsy garb, and gave young beatniks who sought her out the admonition that rebellion had been discovered decades earlier.

ROMANY MARIE
TAVERN

GREENWICH VILLAGE N.Y. CITY N.Y.
20 CHRISTOPHER ST   TEL SPRING O103

JUST SUPPOSE!!!

IN THESE SAD DRY DAYS. MANHATTAN YAWNS
IN GIGANTIC BOREDOM.
BROADWAY AND ITS GARISH LIGHTS?
NO!
THEN WHERE?
THEN WHAT TO DO?
BUT JUST SUPPOSE THERE WAS A PLACE, WITH A
PEASANT ATMOSPHERE?
A PLACE THAT GAVE AN HONEST GLIMPSE OF
"ROMANTIC ROMANIA"?
A PLACE WHERE COALS GLOW ON AN OPEN
GRATE, WHERE, INSTEAD OF JAZZ, COME SOFT
LANGUID, GYPSY AIRS OF THE OLD CARPATHIANS?
A PLACE WHERE ONE SIPS TURKISH COFFEE AND
FRAGRANT DRINKS?
A PLACE SERVING A TABLE - D'HOTE DINNER
OR DISHES SO DELICIOUS THAT THEY TEMPT THE
JADED PALATE?
WHAT THEN?
WOULD THAT AMUSE YOU?
FOR THERE IS SUCH A PLACE!-
ROMANY MARIE TAVERN
AT 20 CHRISTOPHER ST...
GREENWICH VILLAGE, N.Y.C.
TEL. SPRING O103
ONE BLOCK AND A HALF EAST OF THE 7TH.
AV. SUBWAY. CHRISTOPHER ST. STATION; OR
ONE HALF BLOCK WEST OF 6TH, AVE "L".
8T. ST. STATION.

Marie
usually
wore exotic
earrings,
bracelets,
rings and
necklaces of
jade, onyx
and bronze.
(*Photo by
Miro*)

Announcements of the doings at
Marie's Christopher Street place,
accompanied by a photo of Marie
in the romany mode, carried the
notation that "Hand Printing
and Photograph" were by Sasha
Stone, the sculptor who persuaded Marie to join him in Paris
by threatening suicide.

A personally illustrated score and drawings for one of his many wry songs captured the spirit of Bobby Edwards, an Ivy League Marie addict, who sold hand-made cigar-box ukeleles in Marie's places, and invented the punny slogan for bohemian separateness from the mainstream: "Eternal Villageance is the Price of Liberty."

"Do You Remember" Evenings
THREE DAY
REUNION CARNIVAL
APRIL 1-2-3

Dear Friend:

A group of Romany Marie's friends have decided on Thursday, April 1st, Friday, April 2nd and Saturday, April 3rd for a big reunion.

We hereby extend an invitation to you as an old habitue of Romany Marie's and feel sure you will spend a very swell evening among the great, the near-great, the would-be-great, and - thank God - the never-will-be-great; in short, among your friends and the thousand friends of Marie!

Will you kindly send your reservation in now, and state for how many, and for which evening. (Space is limited.)

With greetings from the

COMMITTEE OF SPONSORS

P.S. Your guest of honour -

APRIL 1 - Rockwell Kent

APRIL 2 - ?

APRIL 3 - ?

DINNER - $1.25
55 GROVE St.
TEL — 1PM,- 2A.M. Chelsea 3- 9495

SPONSORS

		ARRANGEMENT COMMITTEE:
LEONARD ABBOTT	ALBERT MOLDAVEN	ANN BUTLER
STUART DAVIS	VILHJALMUR STEFANSSON	ELAINE MASON
PETER FREUCHEN	SAMUEL REICHMANN	KATHERINE YOUNG
KUNIYOSHI	JOSEPH ROBINSON	TOSIA
EDITH HALPERT	ART LANDRY	RICHET
NILES SPENCER	EDGAR VARÈSE	
ROCKWELL KENT		

OLD FRIENDS and PATRONS

Kathleen Millay
George Tobias
Paul Draper
E. E. Cummings
Lionel Stander
Diego Riviera
Orozco
Brancusi
Marcel Duchamp
Leger
Stephen Graham
Conrad Bercovici
Emanuel Kammeroff
Carlos Davila
Cleon Throckmorton
Prince Bibesco
  Nelson O'Shaunessy
  William Bullitt
  Ocario Ootarpus
  Fred Loos
  Theodore Dreiser
  Sinclair Lewis
  Ernest Hemingway
  Helen Westley
  Fanny Ward
Alexander Popini
Margaret De Elvarez
Jack Dean
Eloise McCaskill
Hunt Dietrich
Ben Hecht
Frances Parkes
Harrison Dowd
Earl Hanson
Dr. Rüdiger Bilden
  Hugh Ferris
  Peter Blume
  Malcolm Cowley
  Paul Robeson
  Witter Bynner
  Niles Spencer
Ralph Schofler
Kyra Markham
Jackson Phillips
Carmen Heider
Andree Emery
Jim Harris

David Gaither	Tamiris
Peter Neagoe	Art Young
Edgar Varese	Mary Blair
Ann Butler	Sam Jaffe
Holger Cahill	Edna Aug
Howard Scott	Dr. Angel
Joseph Stella	Fred Kelly

  John Sloan
  Samuel Reichmann
  Albert Muldavin
Bernice Abbott
Buckminster Fuller
Tony Salemme
Dr. Mary Holten
Glenway Westcott
George Frame Brown
Muriel Draper
Cynthia White
Susan Glaspell
Lowell Thomas
  Sir Hubert Wilkins
  O. O. McIntyre
  Arthur Frank
  Charles Norman
Louis Sobel
Edith Corning
Paul Yawitz
Kohana
  Charles Ruggles
  Rose O'Neil
  Edna St. Vincent Millay
John Coffee
Harry Kemp
Bobby Edwards ------
        and many others

A 1939 "revive Marie's" benefit saw an extraordinary roster of stars among the inviters.

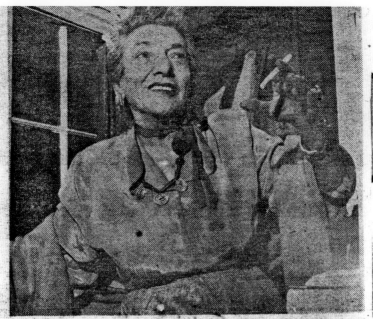

THE LAST OF AN OLD BOHEMIAN. In the place to which she was completely devoted — Greenwich Village — ROMANY MARIE MARCHAND died last week. Widowed for a decade, she spent her last years at the home of Mrs. Bob Brown, wife of the writer, West 8th Street.

—Juster-Cook

Romany Marie:

La Reine Est Morte— There Is No Other

by Mary Perot Nichols

"Yes indeed, yes indeed, yes indeed," the old man mumbled as he shuffled up to the podium. A murmur of remembrance swept through the audience, peopled predominantly by the elderly, as he made his way. He bowed to a few in the group as he went. It was the funeral of Romany Marie and he had come to pay homage. The old lady who never accepted age and kept hers a secret — she was close to 80 — had died two days earlier in her beloved Greenwich Village.

Recalling the lively anarchist days, before Communism had strait-

with full mustache, looking about 80, Bercovici spoke in a quavering voice. "I never looked on her as a character or a Lady Bountiful," he said, making oblique reference to those speakers before him who had told of the many famous writers, poets, and artists who had been fed free of charge by Rom-

The *Village Voice*, then the weekly paper most favored in Greenwich Village, paid special homage in 1961 upon the death of Romany Marie. The obit quoted what Romanian-born novelist Konrad Bercovici said at Marie's funeral: "She was not like the frustrated centipede, she walked on all the hundred feet she had, which was her heart."

seem titanic when not subjected to the glittering contrast of his confreres. No wonder Villagers migrate ruefully uptown into the acclaiming vorteci of wealth and mediocrity."

So much for the clipping. All I can say about it is I think Bobby Edwards couldn't look far enough ahead, to see other new waves coming, because Bohemia is almost always yesterday for the old, but almost always today for the young.

But Bobby was an amusing fellow. Tall, thin, with glasses, a refugee from Harvard, he came around with cigar-box ukuleles that he satirically sang to, and then tried to sell. He made the ukuleles, decorated them beautifully, and plunked away as he sang his songs:

"We are holy Christian martyrs
We don't shave or clean our faces
When we sit in public places
We are so holy that we are sure
That our morals are secure.
Halitosis, halitosis,
Holy Hallelujah."

Bobby Edwards used to sing that. He also had a song about the Boston boys who were opening antique shops in Provincetown.

He lived for years and years on the first floor of an old building on McDougal Street. You couldn't get into the place, he had everything there. He did photography, he composed music, he wrote, he did everything. People used to go in there just out of curiosity, to look at all this accumulation. And there is when he composed his songs.

"I do not care for ladies when they paint, paint, paint,
Their decorations fill me with restraint, straint, straint
For I'd sooner kiss a camel
Than a makeup of enamel,
And that is why I'm living like a saint, saint, saint
(Though some folks may imply I'm not).
I do not care for ladies when they sing, sing, sing,
And show their teeth and gums and everything, thing, thing

For when they gargle a coloratura
My intentions they grow purer,
They're not the sort to which I cling, cling, cling,
I could see them all in Sing, Sing, Sing."

Or:

"The Sultan's wives have got the hives
From eating anchovies and chives
There will be hell.
The sultan's camels have ate banamels
And they're acting like damn fool mammals,
There will be hell! There will be hell!
When the old man from the war arrives,
The sultan's goat has ate his coat,
Thus inadvertently contracting hives.
Allah! Allah!"

It was a rollicking spirit with bite in it. Bobby used to write the song about Lizzie Mossbasket, the belle of Hubert's Cafe-tit-teria. The bite was that he patterned it after one of the waitresses in my place, she was Lizzie Mossbasket. It went like this:

"I know a girl
I'd like to whirl,
I'd like to hurl
Into the river one day,
She's a pest,
Don't give us no rest,
Always asking for pay.
She's the belle of Hubert's Cafe-tit-teria
Down on Sheridan Square
Where the nuts and the bums
With the sex hysteria
Patiently give her the air.
She hasn't a home,

A place of her own,
She domiciles everywhere,
And her name, if you ask it,
Is Lizzie Mossbasket,
The belle of Sheridan Square."

It's one of those things I don't like to tell because the girl is in me, I mean she has a chip on her shoulder.

She was the daughter of a very successful out-of-town professional man who had a lot of clients from New York, and some of them used to bring her to the Village. The first thing, she fell in love and she felt that in the Village one could lead a very gay life, so she left home and took a little room in the Village, wanting to be a Villager, like so many other girls.

Well, if the sightseers would come down and look for the wild girls of the Village, she would be one of them. She was very aggressive, very vivid, gypsy. She dressed colorfully, short hair but she kept it well, kept herself groomed, always looked beautiful, but people had a lot of fun with her, she'd insult them, used a terrible language. She wasn't coordinated with her wildness.

One day her father came in, this distinguished man, said to me he understands his daughter is working for me, waiting on tables. I said I didn't know whose daughter she was but she's a nice little waitress, one of the best we have. If sightseers come in who aren't part of our crowd, she can work up a longer bill than any waitress in the place.

"Well," he said to me, "I want to ask you something. I can't make anything out of her, maybe you can."

So this boy started coming in who said he was going to be a reporter. A funny boy. Used to sit around and make monologues. Spill them out there in the place, and bore us to death with it. Well he and this girl got together, they got married.

They all called him "ham" because he was acting all the time, and I'd say why the hell don't you go out and get a job, look at her, she has to work. I asked her, "Why don't you make him get a job?" Her answer was that she didn't want him to have a job, she wanted him to realize his ambition, to become a movie actor. She was willing to work hard to make him into an actor.

Well, that's something. Love is like art, you do it, you don't talk about it. But one day she came to announce to me that she's pregnant, she can't afford it and wants to do away with it.

I said, look if I know that guy I know that the best thing is for you to go through with it, because he'll say that's my baby, and he'll buck up. You say you want him first to make something of himself. Well I'm telling you that he'll only make something of himself if you give him some responsibility.

She made up her mind. She waited on the tables pregnant, almost until the last minute. She gave birth to the child, and it seems to me almost that same month he broke through for his first little part in the movies they were then producing in New York. Pretty soon they had a nurse and they migrated to Hollywood.

Of course, life is not often fairy tales. After two years she left him, trotted back to the Village. Her story was that he had become high-hat, wanted only to go to places where people would look at him, to the point where she couldn't bear it. The thing is, she opened a shop, became a very fine business woman in the Village, did beautiful painting. Lizzie Mossbasket made it through.

It is one example of what a person makes of hurts in their life. Some people can go through life, be hurt, and turn it into something positive, creative. Others accumulate hurts and then something happens to them, they either go crazy or they become callous and cold and greedy.

Anybody would recognize the name of the fellow in that story but as I say, they are both eating knives about that chapter so I don't like to tell. She has a big chip on her shoulder about it.

The fact is, for years I carried such a big chip toward Puck Durant. For years and years, until one day she said why don't we let bygones be bygones. It came from the time she and I went into partnership together, after several moves of the caravan.

You see, at the same time that Papa Strunsky, the wonderful Village landlord, was fixing up the Waverly place for me, changing five rooms into one big room and giving it to me for $50 a month, I was putting in my bid for a very historic little house. It was called the Garret, it had stood there from the Lafayette days, facing the Washington Square arch.

Well one day a call comes, I can have the Garret now. I wouldn't forego it for the world, and so it was. Carved tables, with people's names on them from years and years. $200 could have it, plus about $40 a month rent.

It was a place that should have been retained as a relic. Hangmen had lived in that place, to oversee the hanging of runaway slaves. It was amazing, the old feeling that was there. The wonderful fireplace, a dining room facing the Arch, and then, three steps down, the mysterious room where I put my piano. And then the hall and there a little kitchen.

I left Marchand with the five cats on Waverly while I took myself over to the Garret. Everything was there, all I had to do was move in. When Grace Godwin had left New York she had given it all over to Honeybell, an Englishman, and he didn't know what to do with it all, he would give it to me.

Well, people adored it. The only thing, the man downstairs was running a store, some kind of a place for ice-cream, also stationery. A Jewish man. When people began to come up to my place—I had many coming—the place would shake.

This man would come to me and shout, "Someday you're going to fall down into my store. You have so many people up there that my light bulbs are dying, you're killing my bulbs." I was frightened to death, thinking this man was going to make trouble for me, how was I going to shut him up?

Well he was doing a very good business down there, so one day I went to him and I said, "Look, I have heart trouble and you're frightening the life out of me. You make me feel as though some day we're going to fall through the floor. I'm going to go tell the building department about it."

No, no, no, he yelled, that would put him out of business. So he stopped, and we were there for two fine years. Only two years because what I didn't know, when we took it, was that the building was toward the tail-end of being programmed to be demolished. Torn down. It should have been saved. Any other country would have done it. But after two years they told me I had to get out, and they tore down the place. New York University got it, and for years it stayed an empty lot.

Well that took me to Minetta Street, 15 Minetta Street. The landlady was a blonde little woman, Miss Abrams, who was married to a Japanese artist, she was so happy to have me there that she did everything in her power to make me comfortable, and people began to flock. Minetta's a side street, it's not Minetta Lane. When you walked in from the real street it was difficult, but people found their way there. Flocks. I was just killed with people there.

But after about a year, on a Saturday night, the place was packed, in came the agent for 62 Washington Square South, one of a row of houses there where he had a restaurant. This agent, Maurice Claremont, a big fat man he was, always used to come into my place, he walked through the crowd to where I was standing in the kitchen, Marchand was just making his big thing of dropping in a pinch of something into the chorba and growling, "Ah, that makes it."

Claremont said, "Marie, I've got something for you. You know my restaurant in Washington Square? I give it to you. A present. The only thing is, you must take it over tomorrow morning, because the girl who runs it is leaving, closing it up tonight, and I don't want it closed even one hour. So it's yours if you take it over right away." My misfortune if I can't, he said, and went away.

It was then four a.m. and he wanted me in a new place by ten. Who should walk in but Mrs. Durant. Puck.

Marie, you're feeling upset. I told her about the offer. She said, "What about me? I'll go and open it for you!" Wonderful!

Well, the reason I tell this story is not because of the opening we had, which was brilliant. Dreiser and all those people came, I brought all my paintings and decorated it. The reason I tell it is not even because of the trouble Puck and I had. This came because when she went to get the place, she signed her name and put up the money, and I was left no choice but to go in as her partner, and we didn't get along. All the columns were mentioning that Romany Marie and Mrs. Durant are pouting at each other.

The causes for that are old history and after all the years it's probably right that nobody should be blamed, although at the time I was crawling into a shell about it. In fact when we broke up, she came to me, "Ever since you decided to leave, I feel I no longer exist. Don't think I'm going to stay here, I'll be in your place all the time." I remember it was pouring rain, and I stood there and told her never mind, don't come.

The reason I am telling this is what it led to, in that when I had left Minetta, I put out the sign saying, "My caravan has moved to 62 Washington Square," but I didn't give up the Minetta Street place. Marchand and I held onto it and lived there. The thing with Puck caused me to return the caravan to Minetta Street, which brought into the picture Bucky Fuller and one of the really amusing highlights of that period of association with the man I think must now be recognized as our nearest thing to a super-scientist evolved right from this American soil.

8. BUCKY AND MARIE

Buckminster Fuller says he met Marie for the first time in 1919, when Betty Salemme took him to Marie's little place on Christopher Street.

"Having come out of the Navy, I was in command of a reserve vessel in Brooklyn, and through this met Vincent Astor who let me have the use of his airplane and thus allowed me to become the first man ever to land an airplane in the state of Maine, an unusual distinction," says Fuller. "Upon Astor's return to New York from a trip of his own, a party obviously was called for, and Betty Salemme suggested the Village.

"We gave it at Marie's, and I recall that Genevieve Pitot, later the accompanist with Martha Graham, got up and danced naked on a table. Very intellectual party.

"But it was the beginning of my Marie experience. Because I went west to Chicago in 1922 and didn't return until 1927, there was a five-year gap for me. Not too long after I got back to New York, Marie was just breaking up with Puck Durant and was setting up again in her own place on Minetta Street.

"I offered to design the décor and furnishings, using aluminum. At least it would help clean up the outside, although I knew I never would have any luck with the kitchen."

It was during that interval in Fuller's symbiotic relationship with Marie that he felt his "concepts were purified" and the beginnings of his extraordinary scientific and philosophical breakthroughs began to take shape, including the three-wheeled car and towered home to which he gave the name "Dymaxion."

"That is why I say my Dymaxion world was born in the world of Romany Marie," Fuller said many years later, adding with a smile, "I do recall it was also the period during which Marie supported Marchand's mistress and a baby they had together."

Marie:

When I left Puck Durant, Bucky Fuller came and said, "Marie, don't worry, I'm going to fix up this place in a Dymaxion way. I'm going to throw out all the old things, and create something new that will have essential character and will lift your spirit."

He was experimenting but it wouldn't cost much, he said. The fact is, it cost plenty. I had to pay about six dollars a quart for that aluminum paint he planned to put on the wall. Well so what, I thought. Bucky is creating for me.

He designed the seats all around the room to be what he said was something like a cross between steamship chairs and aeroplane chairs. I didn't know what he meant by "aeroplane." Anyway, the chairs were made with a frame, but where you sat was canvas, a thick heavy canvas covered with a shiny black oilcloth. I had yards and yards of this canvas. He also made what he called aeroplane tables, with cross-legs under them of aluminum.

All around, for the lights, were like horns of aluminum. The place was so illumined. And because he believed that the things of utility should be integrated, should be in place of any ornamentation, everything was aluminum. I had an elevated area which was painted that way. The water pipes, the heating pipes, they were painted with aluminum so they would be like decorations.

All right the opening night came, a big crowd, including many architects and engineers who recognized his genius but lacked his courage, stubborn courage.

Well right away I had a hardship with the luminosity. Bucky said the idea of having luminosity in the place was so that pseudos wouldn't come and hide in my place, they prefer to go hide in dark rooms, dark dining rooms where you can't see them well—can't see through them. To this room, Bucky said, only real and upright people would come, because you would immediately see all the way through them and they wouldn't mind the test.

The fact was, nobody liked it, and I don't care how real they were. So I had to stand in the middle of the floor and instead of talking about the nice things I have to eat and the good values of being together, I had to explain his philosophy. His philosophy of doing it, instead of the philosophy of a center. Well, that was already a hardship because it was a deviation from my doing. Besides that, the new tables were wiggling when we put food on them.

Well, all right, so everybody is sitting around on those new canvas seats, and while everything is animated, the whole place packed with people—CRASH—the new chairs collapse, the whole house of people fell down. There they were, sitting on the floor. All at once. Those who didn't fall, they were stuck in the chairs, couldn't get out.

It was the most ridiculous spectacle you ever saw in your life. It wasn't enough there was a deviation with all the luminosity—when they sit down, they fall down.

We had to bring out chairs—real chairs—and do what we could that night. And next morning, early morning, I had to have a carpenter make me old benches like I had before.

Bucky said this: "Yes, Marie, it is embarrassing, but it was an experiment. It shows that you were reaching out for modern living and," he said, "it's only natural that in the process of experimentation things like this can happen."

That's the way it was reported in the newspapers, and why should I do anything but forgive him? I was still in the spirit of what Hugh Ferris, the architect, had said to me. Hugh is the one who later designed the theme structures, the trylon and perisphere, for the 1939 New York World's Fair. He had told me, "Marie, if you will give a hand to Bucky Fuller, you will go down in history." And this I believed, but of course the reason I helped Bucky was because of my belief in his philosophy, regardless of the falling down and the luminosity.

"Today's art is a thing that collects dust," Bucky said. "These aluminum things will never catch dust, and we're heading toward a time when there will be no dust collectors.

"Nothing will be static or stagnant, everything will move and be functional."

I could see the truth of his philosophy, and it is what Bucky proceeded to apply in his so-called Dymaxion house, the first model of which he exhibited in my place there on Minetta Street.

His family had thrown him out because they thought he was meshugah. Crazy. His wife, Anne, was a daughter of a great architect of the old school, Hewlett; in Long Island there is a place called Hewlett.

So I carried through with Bucky. One friend gave him a room in the Village and I gave him the food, and Fuller and I began to sit up all night, discussing the philosophy of the future and of living. And he was working on this house model. The poor fellow, nobody wanted to know him.

The house design represented a new living philosophy. It appealed to me very much because instead of breaking your neck carrying in a lot of furniture and other things, his house would have all the furniture and appliances and things integrated into it.

You wouldn't need a lot of property, only enough to allow land space for a tank and a tower, the rest of the house would be in the air, and be held up with cables, like the George Washington Bridge across the Hudson.

Bucky used to take me to look at the bridge when it was in its skeleton stage, and he told me this was the look of the future—everything built of piano cables and wires that would be so arranged to carry any weight, the bigger the structure the more its strength.

As he developed his house model, he showed me that you would elevate yourself into it, and find a house with its own light supply—no more need for power companies and poles. His concept was along the lines of the human body, a mass of center with the cables as the bones and arteries. He had pneumatic floors so there would be no need for bedding, temperature regulation to eliminate the need for coverings. Children would be able to go anywhere in the house and never hurt themselves.

The "servants" all would be in the walls, automatic, eliminating every drudgery. He had new names for the rooms. The living room would be the "state of being" room, where it would be possible to play the level of illumination just like you'd play a piano. The room where you'd work would be the "utility room"—all the appliances, even a blackboard, an adding machine, contained in the wall, you'd push a button and the desired thing would appear as needed.

When the model was finished, he brought it to my place for exhibition, and we had everybody worthwhile come down to examine it. They made it possible for him to travel through the country and display it at architectural schools where they measured it, tested it, found it correct in all its aspects.

Another thing he was doing with me was his Dymaxion car. It looked like an airplane, three wheels and a motor in the back. I rode in that car and was it something! It spun around, made every other automobile on the street look like a carriage. Instead of needing to be turned around, it could revolve.

We went out in it one day and the policeman said we were playing an Irish trick because when we came to a red light Bucky revolved the car so we were going the other way, and there was no law to prohibit such a maneuver.

Naturally, his hope was that these things would be mass produced. His vision of burying the utility things in the walls of the house was so remarkable, so ahead of its time. You press a button, a door opens, you put in your food, it cooks itself. In another opened recess you put in your laundry, it washes automatically.

Fuller wanted the first Dymaxion house that might actually be produced to be placed in the center of a large city, where all strata of people could test its livability. There was a time when the federal government wanted to give him an order for 50,000 Dymaxion houses but landlords and the people in the materials industries fought it, and it wasn't carried out.

When the model was showing there on Minetta Street and people saw the ease of living it would bring, some said to me, "What will we do with ourselves? We won't have work to occupy our time." Of course, the answer to this was we have so many senses in ourselves that are not permitted to develop, creative senses, that this genuine elimination of drudgery will give us the time to develop these senses, to be more creative as human beings. And it would be more than the business of creating "leisure" by cluttering up houses with machines and appliances that stand around and crowd the people space.

Well, the years have begun to show acceptance and use of Fuller's technical philosophy. Everywhere you are going in the world, you are beginning to see his geodesic structures and his Dymaxion principles. And the reason I say Bucky is the nearest thing to a super-scientist that is "all-American" is because that man hasn't had one influence from Europe. Not one. He's descended from one of the greatest women in America, Margaret Fuller, who was a friend of Emerson's, and Bucky belongs to that heritage. Never was he influenced by anything but this American soil.

He actually built several of his Dymaxion cars, and sold a few. The first Mrs. Leopold Stowkowski bought one, and a couple more by movie actors—six thousand dollars a car. Then some auto racers from England came to invest in it, Stefansson brought them. This led to shenanigans being played on Bucky by the automobile industry; they added things to the engine and all that Bucky didn't approve, and one of the racers was killed. But the car wasn't scratched, it was such a massive, such a wonderful car.

So. Real genius, and that is part of what was going on when the feature stories were telling about nothing but degeneracy in the Village in the twenties. This was the usual mistake, of not recognizing that in every vital time you have many layers. There are the degenerates on the edges, and there are the posers and the pseudos, but in the center—if there is health as we had—then you will find a core of people who are operating for new ideas and new concepts because they have a belief in mankind. Their sex habits and their drinking, if they do it, are not ends in themselves, they are coordinated into the main, creative concern.

This one-to-one creative coordination was something I saw develop when a short Japanese came one night into the place in 1927. He had been sent by Brancusi, with whom he had been training in Paris. When you go to New York, Brancusi had told him, do like I and Matisse did, go first to Romany Marie's.

Well, who was this Japanese? It was Isamu Noguchi, and the first thing I did, of course, was push him to Bucky Fuller, who still had that fascination with new materials like aluminum.

Night after night there developed a kinship that you could see influenced the work of the other. It seemed like every time I looked up, there were these two little men talking, talking. And no question in my mind, it was what Noguchi took from Bucky that led him into his period of striking portrait busts in various new metals.

I mentioned the early help to Bucky Fuller from Vilhjalmur Stefansson. Stefansson was also a part of this central core. It is now a matter of history that Stefansson made profound contributions to the knowledge of diet and human society and world geography out of the observations he made from his Arctic explorations and his years of living with the Eskimos.

Stefansson was constantly in my place, often bringing down other members of the Explorers' Club, such as Sir Hubert and Lady Wilkins, Peter Freuchen, Joseph Robinson, Lowell Thomas and so on. There were three people who were fixtures in my place who resembled each other: Stefansson and Marchand and Art Young who had not only a wonderful cartooning talent like Thomas Nast but a high, brilliant intellect and a most marvelous sense of humor. Young did cartoons of me and everybody; women were crazy about him.

Anyway, from the back, Art Young and Marchand and Stef had the same head. Large, strong, bushy, they resembled very well. One of the great surprises in my place was Stefansson acting like a host, talking to newcomers to make them feel at home. Many times these newcomers would come to me and say, "Surely this is not THE Stefansson!" When I would say of course, they would exclaim, "My God, we've wanted to meet him for years, we never expected to run into him here, and find him so friendly."

The thing is that while he always shied away from personal publicity, the greater the success of his life and work, the more he mentioned those things that were his early doing. He never was afraid that talking to just anybody and helping to make my place friendly and warm would hurt his name or his fame.

Yet he rarely mentioned his 1913 Arctic exercise that began as a ten-day hunting trip but kept him away five years, mapping 100,000 square Arctic miles. Many people will remember the year during which he lived entirely on meat to prove his conclusion that an all-meat diet is categorically healthier than a mixed diet. He would come in several times a night to have his meal in the place. He would have a steak for dinner and a piece of chicken for dessert. Then he would go off to give a radio lecture or some such thing, after which he returned to eat some spiced beef. Once in a while he would take tea with it. We could testify that he never ate anything but meat during that entire year, and at the end of the year he was in better condition than when he started. He fulfilled his test.

Stef always would be available in my place until an occasion when people would go to him and say, "Mr. Stefansson, tell us something about the Eskimos."

Then he would look to me for help. Here he was in the place for recreation, and such people were expecting him to tell them about things he'd already written in his books. So when that happened I would say to these people, "Mr. Stefansson has written about 18 books on the Arctic. Have you ever read one? If you keep this up, I will have to ask Mr. Stefansson to make recordings of his answers, so that when you ask him to talk about the Eskimos I will turn on the machine and you can listen."

Stef loved that. It really got him freed.

One night, before he had put in an appearance, I found in the place quietly sitting, having a coffee, a young man who looked like a seaman. A little fellow. People around the table—as I've said, my place was something like a club, when a stranger walked in, the regulars were immediately curious—people around the table asked him from where he came.

He was a little shy. He said, "I come from very far away." They let him go a little while and then somebody turned to him again and said, "Where is the far away?" He said, "Oh, from very far. From the Arctic. Yes, 27 years ago I joined an expedition as an explorer. I went to the Arctic, and I stayed. I married a native girl, an Eskimo, and I have six children with her." Again he retired into his shyness. But then his next comment made everybody perk up their ears.

"There was one man who excited me into joining that expedition. I haven't seen him since, and I'm looking for him." Somebody asked what this man's name was, that he was searching for. He hesitated, thinking he was being made fun of.

Then he said, "Well, it so happens I recently brought my wife to Seattle, the closest place where she could have a lot of dental work done, so I thought I should take the opportunity to come here to New York, maybe I would be lucky enough, by some miracle, to locate the man who made me join that expedition.

Of course we all wanted to know: what is the name of that man? "Oh, you wouldn't know him," he said. "His name is Stefansson."

Well, they all knew Stefansson was coming in that night, so they said, "Have another coffee. Have a bite. People do drop in here so—who knows—this Stefansson might show up." Again he thought he was being joshed. He said, "Oh, I didn't mean that. I'm not such a fool as to think I can just drop into a place and there will be Stefansson." One of the people said, "Well, nevertheless, this is a fantastic place. You never know. He could drop in. Stay and finish your coffee."

Before he finished, in walked Stef. Well, he was always a calm person, nobody ever knew him to get excited. That night was different. He shouted, "Costello! What are you doing here!" The man got up, in complete disbelief, he said, "I don't know. I was passing by this little place, I thought it looked interesting, I dropped in."

Stef cried, "You mean to tell me that from 40,000 restaurants in New York City, you just happened to pick the one that I frequent?" Well, then I jumped up—they were embracing—because Stefansson, being a scientist, did not believe in psychic phenomena. Whenever I talked to him about this, he brushed it off.

I said, "You don't believe in psychic phenomena. Well, this man, having lived with the Eskimos, took on their spirit, their psyche, and that is how he intuitively knew where to find you."

It was Stefansson's turn to jump. He rushed to the phone—he always did the practical, scientific thing—and called the few friends he knew who were in New York, who'd been connected with the expedition, and before that chap Costello returned to the Arctic, there was a tremendous banquet given for him. The celebration with Stef went on for days.

Before Costello said goodbye, I managed to ask about his family, in particular the six children, were they girls or boys? He laughed and said, "Three cooks, three trappers."

Things like that reunion are what held such a lifetime of interest for me in my places. I have seen people meet there who never thought they would meet again. There they were, drawn together by the sheer feeling of a center.

For about 12 years in my place, Stefansson used to see this girl from Brooklyn, Evelyn Schwartz, who was not only very bright but very beautiful. Finally, he invited her to become his personal secretary, which she did, and in a short time he noticed how she was able to absorb all the work she was doing for him. They went off to North Carolina and were married.

I knew quite a number of young men who wanted to marry her, but she preferred Stef, 30 years older though he was. Eventually they went off to live at Dartmouth College, to which he presented his fabulous collection of Arctic books and papers. Not only was she doing creative work—she took many trips with Stef, she flew by herself to the Arctic, she wrote a book about the Eskimos—but she was happy in herself. Until today, she claims it as one of the happiest marriages she ever saw.

Of course, other marriages were made in my places, sometimes without my knowing about it. How many times young women came in, and they'd walk over to me and taking out a pair of earrings from their ears, or something like that, "Here, I want you to have these because when I was a young girl you saved my life." How did I save her life, I didn't even know her!

"Oh yes. Don't you remember, Marie? You gave me advice. I used to come in with this boy and you gave me the advice not to continue with him because he's going to encourage me into a one-sided life that is really false to the spirit of the Village. And now I'm married and I have a baby and I'm terribly happy and I remember every word you said." I suppose there are maybe 20 marriages of this kind I know of.

Naturally, there must be recognition of the nature of marriage. What is it? A dot, just a dot. Unless you can build from there there is no picture, or you build one-sidedly and the picture falls apart.

I know many people did not realize the kind of marriage picture Marchand and I built together. He was brusque with many people, he used to call Stefansson "the iceman." But he respected my freedom, and he had fantastic wisdom. Just one of the things he taught me: his chiropractics. He had a little booklet he found that was called, *A Hundred Stories Your Feet Could Tell.* A little, old book. It told the stories of how, in your body, are connections going down to the feet. When a person came and complained of gallbladder pain, Marchand would tell him to take off his shoes, and then he would feel each of the person's toes and the ankles until, invariably—all of a sudden—"Ouch! I never knew I had a pain there!" Ah, but that's really the pain you feel upstairs, Marchand would say. Press the place in the feet for 15 minutes and the pain upstairs goes away. *A Hundred Stories Your Feet Could Tell.*

Well, Marchand was a busy bee with these and other things all the time. Innovative ideas he was happy with, not really the business things in the places. He was so magnetic to women that it was terrific, but there were times when I had to beg him to go out by himself, do something for himself.

That is how he opened a chiropractic office up on Broadway. I went up there to fix up the office with paintings. He spent four or five thousand dollars on that office, a beautiful office.

But then I noticed when I sent him patients, they came back and said they found the place closed. I found that most of these times, it was because Marchand was on the street corner, looking for somebody who was tired, to take them up and give them a free treatment.

But then one day I went up there to the office and I saw a desk there and I said, "I didn't know you have somebody here helping you."

Well, the story is there had been this young woman coming into the restaurant who was a strange, lonely little woman. She would sit there all the time. She was half-English and half-Indian.

My God, come to discover if Marchand didn't have that woman going up there to his office, and this woman was in love with him, like Sasha Stone was with me.

Marchand said, "This will pass. This woman is pestering me." But she pestered him for five years. And he fought her and fought her. She came to me to ask me—she had the nerve to say to me, "Marie, you've had him long enough, why shouldn't somebody else have him for a change?"

He didn't know what to do with it. He wasn't like me, to know how to manipulate it. He wasn't accustomed to it. So he made a mess of it, and I had to take him out of it. She wanted a baby with him, and she told him she's going to make a man of him. Then, when she said she was going to make a scandal, he gave her money. When I found out, I said, "Ah, I'm not afraid of her scandal."

To her, I said, "Marchand could have 15 women, my dear girl, and they wouldn't touch what there is between us two. I don't care how many women he has."

So she kissed my hand, and called me a lady. It cost money. But that was the end of that. Marchand and I went on to greater experiences.

9. A Colony of Artists

Perhaps it was the fact that the walls and corner tables of Marie's various places were better for the display of paintings and sculptures than were the spaces for declaiming poetry or reading plays. Or perhaps it was the influence on Marie of her early role as a volunteer aide at Robert Henri's art school; after all, his goading and teaching paved the way for the landmark 1913 art show at New York's 69th Regiment Armory and produced many of the painters who over the next forty years were to make American art come of age.

Whatever the cause, among all "her" people Romany Marie always seemed closest to her artists, and gave warm heed to their innovations when most everybody else still considered them aberrations. If artists left the Village, it was with her blessings, for she confidently viewed the entire world as a unified organism, with the Village as one of its nerve centers for creative signals. As in her relationships with Marchand, her only stipulation was that amidst the wanderings there should always be periodic return.

Mark Tobey, who did so well with glass-polishing at Marie's Woodstock summer place and who had first come to the Village in 1911, left it in 1923 to teach art at the Cornish School in Seattle. With "migration" as his self-described leitmotif, he lived for most of the next four decades between London, Switzerland, and Seattle where another Marie disciple, Zoe Dusanne, established the city's first private art gallery and for a protracted period was Tobey's agent there. His national reputation did not begin developing until 1944, and it was 1958 before a top prize at the prestigious Venice Biennale set off a series of international honors not achieved by any American painter since Whistler.

"Our Village—Marie's Village—was a human accident," he recollected at 78. "It couldn't be planned. Especially, it couldn't be planned. The Midwest and the Far West were dull, so to see what life was like we had to go to the Village, where Marie's positiveness and vitality were a boon. Nobody much wanted our art, all we had was each other. The Village then was like a sun that went across the horizon and died; we just happened to be in its orbit."

But in 1929, when the Wisconsin-born Tobey was ready after 12 years for his second one-man show in New York, it was Marie's Minetta Street place that provided the locale. "Interior of gallery designed by Buckminster Fuller," said a 1962 volume on Tobey. The show was not a success, but Alfred Barr's viewing of it led to Tobey's inclusion in a Museum of Modern Art exhibition of "Painting & Sculpture by Living Americans." This, and a 1930 major article on Tobey by Marie's longtime friend, Muriel Draper, were vital milestones in Tobey's road to recognition.

Said painter Stuart Davis who, unlike Tobey and some others, remained a Village resident, "From astoundingly different backgrounds, each of us was accepted by Marie with that rare gift of individuality.

"From early on, I was a daily patron of her places and when I was without money, which was often, she would buy one of my paintings off the wall. She operated at some kind of universal, human level. She could take on anybody, talk to them all night, and they'd feel they had a friend."

Yet, said another of Marie's boys, painter DeHirsch Margules, it was "hard to describe her truly, because you could never tie her down to anything anticipatible. She was mercurial. She could be gracious, kind, benign—as good a friend to artists now much renowned as any they can claim—but she could also flail, literally flail those she felt had not done justice to a particular kind of trust."

Although Davis did a painting of one of Marie's places, neither he nor Margules did portraits of Marie. But Tobey and John Sloan did—and so did Robert Chanler, Stanley Ranski, Olaf Olsen, "Chuck" Adams, Clinton King, Walter Houmer, Louise Bromack, Ben Benn, Antonio

Salemme, Oronzo Gasparo, Gladys Brown (Mrs. Arthur Ficke), Julian Levi, Lela Cornell, Anna Neagoe, Joseph Pollet, Toscha Rochet (Mrs. George Yanitelli), Lucy Stander, Sari Kryzanowsky (Mrs. Knud Laub), Leon Tahcheechee, Pauline Schubert and Thomis De Vitis—among others! There was also a bronze bust of her by Judith Simmons, and a striking, full-length photo portrait by photographer George Platt Lynes; he was the brother of Harper's Magazine editor Russell Lynes, and the Richard Avedon of the twenties.

Edith Halpert, operator of New York's Downtown Gallery, said, "When artists came back from Europe the first stop always was Marie's, and with even some uptowners coming in with their troubles, there were always screaming fights going on, usually about the critics.

"Marie fed so subtly, and that earth mother quality of hers was really so earthy, but often some really insensitive bastards came to feed on it. Marsden Hartley was always invited to sit at a special table but as far as I could tell, when he was able to pay his own way, he went someplace else, like the Jumble Shop."

But the Hartley kind notwithstanding, Marie's place always looked like a Left Bank art gallery. Said Buckminster Fuller, "I don't think anybody could estimate how many paintings and sculptures were done of Marie or given to her. But many of these were later lost or dissipated because Marie would get hard up, or because Marchand would sell them so he could buy more books or materials for his odd inventions. Piece by piece, there went for a song what might otherwise have become one of the world's great private art collections."

Marie:

Yesterday, and also today, the sad thing about art is that too many people react to it like they do to a lot of their fellow human beings. Fast. Superficial. Especially if it's something new to them, or different, they take one look and say, "Oh, I don't like it. Oh, what's it mean?" Or they go to the other extreme, especially if it's something flashy and they like to be in with a smart bunch, and they scream, "Oh, wonderful! Oh, fantastic! Oh, I adore it!"

How much do they try to find out about it? Do they investigate a little to try to see how much of a person's nature is in a piece of art, and how honestly is he trying to say something worthwhile about the world? If he's got funny sex habits, have such habits acted to clear his vision about the rest of the world, or cloud it? Or does it have anything at all to do with the goodness of his work?

Too often, none of this. People look and they pass an opinion. Now, I hate to talk about myself, as most people know. If I have a good head, and it works well, I like it to show without my having to say so.

The reason I mention this is that there were times when I fooled myself. A few times. Some people are very shrewd and clever so that even when you take time to consider, they blind you. Let's say they have a vivid vitality. They flash it before you.

They kind of trick you in with all that. I was tricked—both with men and women. In fact, I found myself sometimes arguing with doubters who would say about a certain painter, "Oh, there'll never be anything worthwhile out of that one." And I'd say, any person with such vitality, look, I have hope for them. But in a few years I'd discover they were putting the vitality into fad or fakery, or just plain sexing around, bumming around, not generating. To the contrary, degenerating.

The fantastic genius of Robert Henri was that he could shake up so many developing artists to make the fresh, deep investigation of the American life around them and put its deeper meanings into their art. No more hot-house art, no more comfortable superficiality. No more stereotypes about black people, red people, poor people, odd people.

I should mention that the reason Isadora Duncan came into my place the very first time was that she came to meet Henri, who was at that time the greatest living artist in America. Travel through America and ask the man in the street, "Who's your greatest artist?" They'd say: Robert Henri. Well anyway, some men in the street.

I wouldn't say which of the painters fooled me. Neither would it be right for me to say in detail which painters at one or another time ate free in my places. After all, I didn't make a point of it. I had many paintings in exchange for food, but I don't like to mention that either.

I can mention DeHirsch Margules. I remember a time—a whole period, every painting—he needed help. He was a reporter, a night police reporter, on the *City News*; he used to watch every second he had away from his work, treasure every second, to do a painting. He was passionate for every minute he could grab, weekends or when he got a vacation. He was so intense that he would take a train on the paper's time so he wouldn't lose any of his own time from his painting.

I gave him his first exhibition in my place on Minetta Street. I remember I opened it up and I sold a painting of his to some rich woman. Well, he used to come in with his paintings and he'd say, "Here, I have another one, will you give me food for it?" So I had quite a collection. He's very well known now.

I had a few more like that—names I won't mention because it wouldn't be fair. In Paris, great painters were proud to be mentioned that way, but here I had occasions when some of them would say to me, "If I catch you telling anybody...!!" The late Joe Stella felt this way.

Oh, there was a one! He was one of the "Intelligents" among the painters, but what pleased him most was when his landlord installed an indoor toilet in his Village flat. Everybody who went to visit, he had us pull the new toilet chain.

In his art, he had a gentle touch. He specialized in painting bridges as everyone knows, achieved a marvelous stained glass effect. Later on, poor man, he was very strong for Mussolini. Once, he attended a Carnegie Hall meeting in the thirties, sponsored by the League Against War and Fascism.

When he took his place on the platform, he looked around and saw a sign attacking not only Hitler but Mussolini. He shouted, "Those bastards! They can't put Mussolini in the same class with Hitler." He jumped up and left the hall.

Well, so he came in one night and said he was going back to Italy. "I'm going to paint my people," he said. "Mussolini loves art and artists." Ooh, did he discover different. He came back to America in less than a year, and hid from the world in embarrassment. In Rome, he'd found Fascist guards around the museums. In his hometown nearby, he was told that his family property belonged to Mussolini and the state. And after he'd painted his countrymen the authorities told him, "You painted them here. Here they stay."

Anyway, in quite another category where it came to paintings was dear Niles Spencer. Niles gave me paintings. Many others did the same. Naturally they sat around in the place for almost nothing, they'd sit nights and drink coffee, but they were not in need any longer. I got paintings from them just being grateful that I had a place for them.

By contrast, I had a very interesting thing happen to me with Marsden Hartley. He never gave paintings—he was never known to give anybody a painting. But there was a man by the name of Alfred Steiglitz, that great photographer. Steiglitz had a gallery, and for years while Hartley was in Europe Steiglitz took care of him. Marsden used to send Steiglitz his paintings and Steiglitz would accumulate them and stage exhibitions.

Every year, when Marsden's pictures arrived, I would be there to look at the exhibition. There wasn't a time I missed. Well one of these times, when Steiglitz already was quite ill, he came over to me and said, "I have never seen such an interest as you have. Year in and year out I see you, always coming to Marsden's exhibitions. Did he ever give you a painting?"

I said, "Why should he give me a painting? I have them here, why do I have to take them home? As long as I have the privilege to see them isn't that sufficient?"

He said, "No, I'm going into my own collection and send you a painting of Marsden's. Just a reward."

Next day Steiglitz—DeHirsch was another of his disciples by the way—sent me from his collection a beautiful Hartley painting of high mountains. Years later, when Marchand was sick, I had to sell it, and I am sorry I had to. It was a landscape Marsden did in Santa Fe.

Well I hung it—it was a large painting—and Marsden came back to New York and was coming every night to my place to sit by me—I had a big desk and he had a chair right near me—and Marsden came in—sat himself down, then suddenly looked up and said, "Where did you get that!"

"Not from you!" I said laughing, because he was very stingy. He turned colors in the face. Then I told him, "It was a reward for looking at your pictures."

It was his turn to have a little smile, and he said, "It's one of my best pictures."

More or less in the same way is how I got the portrait that was done of me by Stanley Ranski, a very well known Polish painter who also painted a lot of the faculty of Columbia University. I guess he was one of about 30 who did things of me. Perhaps one reason some of them were interested is that I would work with the artist the minute I began to pose for them. I wasn't just a model, I immediately cooperated.

Namely, how? When you start posing for an artist, you've got to make up your mind that you will go to the finish. That's number one. Then you've got to make up your mind that you must watch the mood of the artist, so you won't disturb him. You've got to watch his sensitivity, not be asking him every minute, "Oh I'd like to see what you're doing." Many times I posed for an artist for months without once seeing the work. Sometimes, if he would invite me to look at it, I said, "No, I will see it when you have the work finished."

I will say there were only a few who stimulated me mentally while I posed. The rest of them were like dumb. Some artists are not capable of being large enough to be absorbed in their work and also to be doing something else. A few are interested in other things, and while they work they will tackle other subjects.

John Sloan, for instance, had an active social conscience, and there wasn't a subject he wouldn't talk about while he painted and it didn't disrupt him. Others, they couldn't say boo without being disrupted. They are people who paint, period. Nothing else. So are they great people? Yes, some of these did worthwhile things.

One man I posed for—I wouldn't mention his name—he used to go into a trance when he painted. It would frighten me. His eyes would bulge out and he would go into a trance when he looked at me and saw something that interested him. "Hold it! Hold it!" he'd say, and his eyes would bulge. He'd come over to me when he said "Hold it!" so that sometimes I thought he was going to choke me. So much so that I told Marchand to come with me and sit in a corner.

On the other hand, Julian Levi and Robert Henri and Mark Tobey and people like that—I could count on one hand—to them I could hardly wait to go because there I went to further my interest as well as to pose, and it was a joy.

But was I satisfied with the product afterward? Most of the time no.

Did I feel myself in the painting after it was done? No, most of the time, no.

Why did so many people paint me? Oh, ho—in many instances by looking at the last painting that had been done of me and exclaiming, "Ha! This is not you, Marie! I'll show you how it should be done properly."

Perhaps the reason is that I have so many different sides in me that it makes me a strange kind of personality. The kind that in action—moving—gives one impression, and in repose quite another. Some stage people said I should be on the stage because they found me so changeable in personality that I could take on a variety of roles. Of course I like to think that while I change outwardly, inwardly, intrinsically I'm one.

Anyway, outwardly, I could get a change of costume and be a different person. The artists said I could look like a dirty gypsy and I could look like a duchess and I could look like a worker. So, with paintings, also with sculpture and photography, each artist caught a different side. Ivan Black, the publicist, took a picture, I could pass as a society woman; Gjon Mili, who pioneered the stroboscopics with *Life*, he showed an entirely different person. And with my various changes of hair—well, the Englishwoman whom Hemingway made into his heroine in *The Sun Also Rises*, Lady Brett—she came up with still another person. You put the various portraits and photographs side by side, there aren't two people making the same picture.

So I say each one got some of me, but nobody caught it all. Stuart Davis criticized Levi's portrait of me. Stuart said where was my structure, because my height is only about 5 feet one-and-a-half inches but many times I look like a tall woman. I give that impression, Davis said, that illusion.

Well nobody caught that. Nobody caught that I am intrinsically a relaxed person. People that saw me in my place, where I'd be running from one person to another, got the impression I'm like a running sea. Like Joseph Pollet, the Sloan protégé, he painted a large portrait showing me practically falling off a chair. He had the idea that because I got up all the time, he should make me a jumping jack, not realizing that when I sit down for two minutes I relax because I'm relaxed inside.

Each one, they conjured up an image of me before they went to work on it. Sloan said he saw me as a little earthy girl coming to the American shores to put myself over and who got herself on everybody's lips, so that is what Sloan painted. Marvelous—but a quiet, strict looking little girl, whereas Levi's looks like a little refugee woman. Ransky did an idle woman, one who looked like she never worked.

Give it to Tobey, he had a little more of what I'd call true palpitation in his—but still not me. I mentioned Bob Chanler's incurable involvement with Lena Cavalieri, that opera singer—naturally, when Chanler did me he did a cross between Cavalieri and some old gypsy in Spain that he'd wanted to paint all his life, and I reminded him of her.

Tony Salemme did a bust of me that he sold to the Brooklyn Museum. It was the time I was moving the caravan to a place on Eighth Street and I was preparing a big opening, so Tony said he would go to the museum and ask them to send the bust for a week of exhibit at the place.

They were very sweet about it, it was a large thing but they crated it and sent it over, and I put it on the platform I had there where the people used to perform, placed it there so that when people came into my place they saw that.

Well, it was frightful. It didn't look like a live creation of me, it looked like a petrified me.

Sure it looked something like me, and Tony is a great artist and a marvelous human being, but he did a petrified me. There I was—no more action in this world.

You couldn't say the same thing about the work many of these artists were doing on other subjects. By the time I was in the Minetta Street place, many of them already were moving ahead to what is called "abstract" and this meant they were reaching for reality beyond just its surface. I say it was "called" abstract because people did with it what I've said they usually do. They refused to look long enough.

These are the people you could hear saying they didn't like nature. They didn't like going to the country. It bores them, they don't like the quiet, they don't like the new kinds of noises you hear amid the quietness, they don't like something. And these were the people who, when some of my artists went to Woodstock, or to Gloucester, Massachusetts where for several summers Marchand and I also went, and the artists came back to paint the essence of a tree or a field, these people had the nerve to say it wasn't nature.

They missed the point that the first attraction to a thing like that is very much like a love for people. When do you get to really know people? When do you reach the point of being truly able to express something about them? You never reach an understanding until you exercise a real interest.

The same thing with art. If more people would make a point as I and others did, of going around to look at abstract art for 40 years, they would find suddenly a great realism in it. A great realism if you strain for the impression the artist is expressing instead of looking for the details of which a thing is familiarly composed. It's like going to look at the nails and the toes of a person; if you do that you miss their character and the character is the important thing that a person brings.

I must say that, in the beginnings of abstract art, it shocked me, like a person with great complexity would shock me. I knew I had to break through something I felt. But it attracted me, it drew me enough to go over and over again.

I must say it did start me out to a good man, and that's Stuart Davis. How this happened was that when I had the father of abstraction, Leger—the great father of abstraction from Paris, and wonderful! Oh God!—Leger walked into my place, there was a man here in New York who used to bring all these French artists, he's dead now, Broomer, of the Broomer Gallery, he himself was an artist, he brought everybody to me who was to exhibit in New York from Europe.

Well, as I say, when Leger came in, he walked straight over to one of Stuart's paintings, and he looked at it and looked at it. Finally he said, "This is your greatest American abstract art."

Stuart Davis' own character itself was abstract. When you'd go into his studio, when you'd look into his life, you'd see that. Looking at a person or looking at a tree, there is what you see superficially, there is what you see in physical, scientific detail, but there also is an inner feeling, an inner culture that you've got to learn how to look at.

Artists like Stuart wanted to make a statement of their feelings about this inner character. He, in particular, wanted to make a statement about space and balance. I remember when he began his Eggbeater series that brought him the first kind of attention he deserved. For a year, he painted an eggbeater, a fan and a rubber glove nailed to a table. He did also a Socony gasoline pump and a seltzer bottle.

Stuart didn't have any special love for beaters or seltzer bottles. He simply used such things in the center, to make a balance of a piece of canvas, to show that balance and space make up life. People were so puzzled that some years later he went to the trouble of explaining it in words, in a little book in which he inscribed a copy to Marchand and me. Stuart pointed out that without a tremendous idea of the distance between two points, and all the space phenomena connected with this, people couldn't leave the house without being run over. Yet, some of these same people would complain that parallel black lines in a Mondrian painting didn't look like a tree. Such people, Stuart said, wouldn't quiver at the fantastically abstract things science was showing in "reality," yet would continue to expect the artist to go on living in the world of the Mona Lisa.

It intrigued Stuart to be my friend because we were both seeking knowledge of position. What is the artist's position in space, in relationship to the picture he is about to paint? Where are you in relation to the people you truly wish to know and affect?

There was that summer in Gloucester, when Stuart was coming into my place looking glum and despondent, down in the mouth. Temporarily, he didn't have the morale for painting. He could find no motivation.

Now I knew that from Stuart's mother toward him was a love that sometimes was too close for comfort. Too possessive. Well, I thought of the two girls I had staying with me. Would he like to have them sit for him? They came out and were introduced. Davis brightened, and arranged for the two to come to his studio the next morning.

As it turned out, he painted the one with the handsome face. The reason was, he already was so emotionally stirred by the other girl. She was a person who had been infatuated with her artist-brother, used to sit up at nights in Washington Square, alone, just looking at the lights of the studio where her beloved brother lived.

The upshot of that summer was not only that Davis found the *raison d'etre* for painting again, but decided to marry the girl. His mother came rushing to me, frantically bitter and upset. Her Stuart mustn't get married, it was my fault. I asked her, "Do you want everybody to believe you love your son so that you can't bear to have him go to another woman?"

Well, the girl took over the mother's role. Stuart's art was her life, his paintings were their children. Anybody criticizing his work caused her to froth at the mouth. Then, one day, she learned she was pregnant. This must not complicate Stuart's life, his devotion to his work. So she did this, and that, she didn't have the baby, she died.

Years later, Stuart met Roselle, a pale, inwardly-starved girl with a marvelous spirit. She and Stuart found in each other the sort of understanding and love he had known with his first wife. They were married, and she bloomed.

So, just recently, a knock came and I opened the door. And there stood Roselle, Stuart's wife, dressed in black and she looked strange. She looked like herself, yet not like herself.

Is that you Roselle? Yes, she said.

And I said, "What is there about you?"

"I'm having a baby," she said. She was up with the baby.

I almost dropped. Twenty-five years they're married, and I never thought—well, in fact their ideas were that they shouldn't have babies, and they always ridiculed artists who had babies.

She said, "It's an accident, but a good accident. I've decided to let it come. Stuart is a little embarrassed, but he'll get over it."

Well, I looked at her, and I said, "It will be a boy." How could I know that? I told her I never had predicted such a thing without it's coming true. I also had a feeling, I told her, that a very lucky thing was going to happen, something marvelous, when the baby boy is born.

Weeks and weeks went by, and it's strange—on the very day it occurred to me to telephone and see how Roselle was, Stuart answered to say that Roselle had just gone to the hospital. The baby was a boy, and the day after it was born Stuart got the top Guggenheim award, worth $5,000.

But on the day I was supposed to go and see the baby for the first time I didn't go because they telephoned me to say that Niles Spencer had dropped dead. One of the great American painters, I mentioned he was among those who were pupils at the Ferrer School.

He was only about 53, and always a glowy person. He was never sick but he'd had pneumonia and the pneumonia had touched his heart, he'd been in the hospital a few days for observation and came out and was sitting and reading when he died. The day of his funeral was my birthday. The whole art world was there, because he was adored by everybody. He was a pet, because he was so gay and sweet and, as I say, glowy.

Only about a block from the Metropolitan Museum was the funeral parlor, and there Niles was lying dead while in the Museum were two magnificent paintings of his. And when I came back to my place, there were people waiting at the door with flowers for my birthday.

I felt again the basic principle. Life and death are one, and art and people, and nature and time and space, are one when they are properly and deeply related.

That brings it back to Stuart Davis, and to some of the others I had who always fought against being called abstract because what they had was rather a deeper way of expressing realism. Reality.

To be able to have the insight to express reality and then to live with it is not always a happy thing. There was another chap from whom I had paintings, a very good friend of mine, Red Robin. He was a pure-blooded American Indian, a Zuni. From Arizona. He had a big thing with Paula, one of my waitresses. I never had anybody waiting on tables who wasn't part of the place in spirit, and so it was with Paula. She never felt she worked there, on nights when she had to go dancing or posing—whatever she did, she was a little artist in her soul—she would come back afterward and wait on tables as though it was her place.

Anyway, Red Robin. He used to work at the Museum of Natural History, lecturing and doing folklore things. He was a very cultured Indian who had a very hard time, not being able to adjust himself here with white people that he still had a hurt about.

The white people did him dirt, took his culture away from him. Took all his native culture and yet when he went back to his own people he didn't fit in with them either.

So one night he was volunteering to help out at the place and some man I'd never seen before was calling constantly, "Red. Hey, Red," when he wanted something. He was saying it demeaningly. Well, Robin was getting angrier and angrier. Suddenly he leapt at the man and began to choke him. What's to do? I can't prevail against Robin's strength and neither can Marchand.

Nearby was sitting photographer Gjon Mili, quietly reading a paper and eating, paying no attention to the commotion. At the crucial time, when the poor man was beginning to turn colors from the choking, Gjon put down his paper, calmly walked over and began to kiss Red Robin. He started at the hand, proceeded up the arm to the shoulder, then did the same thing on the other side. Robin's grip relaxed, and finally he let go completely and walked away.

I went over to thank Mili who had quietly returned to his seat and was again eating, and reading his paper. He looked at me and said, "I don't know what you are talking about. I haven't done a thing. I've just been sitting here, eating my dinner." Of course that left me free for the important thing, which was to go over and let Red Robin talk himself out.

Even people dear to me would say, "How can you stand to live among such unruly people?" My answer would be that I'd rather live among unruly people who attempt to get under the skin, than among smug people who go to work every morning. You can expect the worst sometimes, but you know you will never miss the best.

This came to me freshly a few years after Mark Tobey's exhibition at my place, when he and I and some others went to Mexico and there I had a marvelous reunion with Diego Rivera and Orozco—great Mexican painters—and with Carlos Chavez, the composer. The thing is, we went by ship and it was the same ship from which dear Hart Crane, the young poet, threw himself into the sea. When that happened I thought of the gray sea, and of the times Crane would come quietly, to talk out dreams and nightmares he was too sensitive to manipulate.

With these vibrations around, it was not possible to live ordinarily. Yet would you believe it, one night there came into the place two Columbia University professors who watched for a while, then called me over and said, "How do you make contact with people? You seem to be able to reach right out and capture the interest and spirit and attention of all kinds. We worry about this sort of thing in our work with students.

Sometimes we make contact, sometimes we don't."

They said, "We've been watching you. You're always *en rapport*, yet you've never studied psychology or teaching techniques, you've never had training."

I had to tell them it was simple. "I'm interested in the people I talk to," I said. "It's as simple as that. I want to give them something. And I want to respond to what they have in themselves. Isn't that what teaching is? Bringing out what is inside of each personality?"

They agreed. But then one said, "Oh, but at what a sacrifice! To do that a person must always be giving of himself."

How do you like that? I said to them, if it means sacrifice to you, you shouldn't stay in teaching. I get nourishment and enrichment from it. Every new person for me is a new experience. That's why I can look fresher at three in the morning than I do when I start.

10. A CAST OF CHARACTERS

What new phenomena could the 1929 stock market collapse and the great Depression of the thirties bring to Greenwich Village, where spartan need had long been a badge proudly worn? John Sloan did a cartoon showing a tattered banker jumping into a shellhole marked "Depression" only to find it already occupied by an artist.

"What are you doing here?" Sloan had the banker exclaim, to which the artist responded, "Why, this is my home."

Marie's next two locations during these years, on MacDougal Street and then on Eighth Street west of Fifth Avenue (still in many ways a main drag of today's Village), sustained the same old lure. Marxism, and railing against economic deprivation, regained as table themes some of the popularity they had enjoyed 15 Village years earlier, but soon gave way to resurgent mysticism, some of it linked to Whitmanesque Americanism. One habitué of Marie's recalled seeing Marchand sidle up to a patron known for his loud defenses of Stalinist purges, to hiss in a stage whisper, "Don't worry, Comrade, everything will be all right with Russia!"

Twice, Eleanor Roosevelt staged benefit parties at Marie's for artists to whom hunger no longer was a creative yardstick. These affairs, according to composer Varese, who remained a Village resident until his death in 1966, were illustrative of Marie's role through the thirties as an adroit and often unsuspected organizer of assistance.

Perhaps predictably, a tall, part-American Indian named Howard Scott made Marie's his favorite lair for planning the development of the movement he labeled "Technocracy" that proposed turning over the American economic system to the engineers and threatened for a time to become a major political factor.

Burl Ives, the folksinger turned actor, said Marie's was for him "an eye-opener, a haven and a blessing to a kid from the Midwest.

"Sometimes Marchand played like the Swami from Bengazzi, he was the only doorman in town who could say hello in 30 languages," Ives said. "And then there was that unforgettable lady who was Marie's mother, a personification of serene wisdom.

"It's always been more fun to sing for a few people than to many, and Marie's had an atmosphere for that, although let's face it, I didn't have a choice in those days. There was a certain purple something about the atmosphere at Marie's, and she herself kept showing her insight into truths about people. She also had a great sense of story—of story in capsule which is what characterizes so many of my favorite songs."

Author Maxwell Bodenheim remained on the scene, mostly pursuing the trail of drink and fornication that led not only to dissipation of his talent but finally, in the mid-fifties, to a brutal death with his mistress at the hands of a demented drifter whose dingy flat they were sharing. However, Bodenheim had the insight in the thirties to perceive that some of those Village alumni whose uptown success went unaffected by the Depression still stayed tied to their Village genesis. He gave the graduates pretty short shrift.

Of novelist Fannie Hurst, Bodenheim said in an autobiography published after his death, "The Fannie Hurst one met in her Central Park West apartment gave the first impression of a stony-faced Cleopatra, poured into a tight velvet gown like cement and smiling coldly down as she wrapped her regal arms around a brace of Persian cats.

"This was not the same Fannie Hurst who was an habitué of Romany Marie's, who laughed heartily at the scalding, satirical humor of Marie. At Marie's, Miss Hurst was like the marble Galatea who was given life by the touch of Aphrodite, the Venus-touch of the Village which thawed many frozen statues and filled their veins with the hot blood of experimental living."

Marie:

Marchand and I always talked about how much more energy there
is in people—in a country—everywhere—than is used, until an
emergency comes and the energy has to be used, it is freed. Of course it
is a terrible thing to have to see tribulation before this dormant energy
comes out, but the way that it came out during the Depression made it
a real moving time to live through.

There were those who made it out just by being shrewd. Like that
Michael Romanoff who went to build such a fortune with a restaurant
in Hollywood. Prince Michael Romanoff? Prince! He was a little tailor
with a never-used riding habit who knew how to treat women, and he
could pass like a prince because women are excited by the sight of a
riding habit. After all, my Marchand used to have one. And there were
plenty of uptown women who remained rich during the Depression
and who would go running after their own kind of escape. Either they
were going to a plastic surgeon for a face-lift or to a psychoanalyst for a
soul-lift.

But I am talking about other kinds of people. I am talking about
those who were right in the middle of life. There was a man who had
backed the little theatres. He backed the Provincetown, he backed the
Washington Square Players. He remained a millionaire, a great
philanthropist. He sent word to me to come, and he asked me how was
I carrying on, what with so many people not working. He said they
were flocking in on him and asking for help and all that. Not only
asking, he said, they were invading him.

Naturally, I told him that I have no money, but so long as I have
food on my stove, I'm willing to share with those who need it.

He said, "Well, we really have the same kind of shop. You are ready
to give, in your way, and I am ready to give in my way." And the upshot
was that he arranged every now and then to provide money I should use
to arrange not only food but little loanings for 20 of the artists and
writers that I believe in. He did that several times. The people didn't
even know. He didn't want me to tell them and I didn't want them to
feel—well, I made them always feel that they were entitled to it.

And like always, the seriously-working writers and artists were seeing further ahead and deeper than the rest of the people of the times. They were seeing through the Depression, they were seeing past the rise of dictatorship in Europe.

How many interesting people were coming to the place! How many interesting things there were to talk about! I remember Clifford Odets, just a kid hanging around to get a few words from Harry Kemp.

Odets went on to write his plays that said if people will be good to each other then a society will catch its breath and survive.

When the federal government started the WPA artists' project, and also the writers' project, they were intended to provide work for unemployed creatives but, believe me, they did a great deal more. A great deal. My place was beaming with new interests through these projects. The most amazing energy came forth, a real demonstration of how an emergency time leads to new discoveries. Every time I saw a new life feeling in my place in those times, I discovered it was being produced by an interest in those WPA projects.

Writers who had been hanging around the Village and who hadn't been working for years—they had sunk into stagnation, they had sunk into sleeping all day and hanging around the cafés all night—suddenly they were like being called to arms.

Orrick Johns was the first New York head of that project, the writers' project—people really should go back and read his poetry, a fine poet—and Johns went to the government and said, "I'm confronted with a bunch of raving maniacs. They haven't worked for years, now it's hard to stop them. I need some psychiatric attention for them before I can put them to work." He did, he got a psychiatric consultant and before long he began to have the most magnificent results out of it.

Maxwell Bodenheim was in it. Nobody, no person could open up their vistas to work because they weren't accustomed anymore, but the WPA did it, that opened it up. John LaTouche, who wrote the "Ballad for Americans," that's where he wrote it, on the WPA Project, with Earl Robinson doing the music:

In seventy-six, the sky was red
Thunder rumbling overhead,
Bad King George couldn't sleep in his bed,

And on that stormy morn,
Ol' Uncle Sam was born!

LaTouche was a little fellow from Virginia who started writing poetry in Columbia University and got a prize there. He wrote that Ballad during the project and nobody wanted it at first, but look what happened later, when Paul Robeson sang it. So, Robeson became Communistic. So? Sadly, that is how he found to handle his hurts because there was then hardly anyplace in America outside the Village where you wouldn't look twice because a white woman and a black man were walking hand in hand. Robeson's vision was clouded by this indignity.

Anyway, the new energies of people like LaTouche were called out. Head of the Art Project nationally was a dear man, Holger Cahill. He was doing art criticism for John Sloan in the Brooklyn Museum years back, he had enough knowledge of art, and a great interest in art.

When the art project was going, Stuart Davis came in one day all laughing, he said, "With a weekly paycheck of $23.83, I've got security for the first time in years!"

Cahill did a remarkable thing, he took tours into all of the hidden, backwater places of America to determine what had been done in art, what was possible. There always had been a rumor that America had no art. And Cahill discovered a great deal, even of early American art—crafts. He went to God-forsaken, out-of-the-way places, like Omaha and places like that, and he discovered young men who weren't calling themselves artists—they were railroad men and cowboys and such—but they were doing some wonderful things in art.

When Cahill would look around such towns and didn't see any gallery, invariably he'd go to the town banker and say, "Look here, I'm the head of the Art Project, and I've discovered that you have here in your town people who are making efforts to create art and they don't even have a gallery where they can go look at great art." Cahill ended up by having nineteen bankers in nineteen little God-forsaken towns lead in financing the building of galleries.

And in the Village, in the place, we were feeling the marvelous impact of all this generation. Edith Halpert, with her very successful gallery uptown here in New York, when she went to Washington to see there the exhibition of art collected by Cahill during the project, she said, "I've got to have a finger in this pie."

She was so excited, she came to tell us about the artists she'd picked for her gallery, to help sell their later work. It was a terrific discovery, that if there was a fathering of what was being done artistically in this country, it would be worth studying, indeed they would come from Europe to study here.

I can't say enough about how the talents and energies that might have remained dormant were stimulated during that period, it was one of the most significant periods to live through. A whole new outpouring, in music, in writing, in ideas of architecture and design.

And all this was intensifying the hunger for a center, the same as in the earlier years. As poor Max Bodenheim once said, in thinking of the book by Carson McCullers, *The Heart Is A Lonely Hunter*—as long as the heart is trapped in isolation and unable to join the wild chorus of being, it must have a familiar meeting place where it can seek other hearts like it.

Burl Ives came into my place in rags almost, with a guitar in his hands. He was Beryl Ives then. He was brought by the International Folk Festival, he played the guitar for them. I went over to him and said, "Look, I'm terribly moved and touched by your music, why don't you make yourself more known?" Of course, he laughed, he was still at dead ends. But he began to come regularly, and there he met photographer Gjon Mili, who helped make Ives famous.

After he became known, he continued to come in and he would eat five chorbas one after another—he's very fat, you know—he so loved that chorba. Later, when he played the first time in *Oklahoma*, he sent by Western Union two tickets for me to sit in the orchestra. Another time, when he had a recital, he played in Town Hall and sent me tickets, people were standing in line to get in, you thought God knows what important event is going on.

Ives fell in love with a charming girl, quite well off, and when they were to be married, they came to Marchand. Marchand said to her, "He's a fine man, he won't hurt you. Just don't hurt him."

The thing about Ives and a lot of the others, many not well-known, others known, like Odets, Eddie Albert, Orson Welles, Saroyan, they were a new generation growing up between the two world wars, they were prepared to deal energetically with new challenges as they arose. But this is not to say that the older group, who were born early enough to have felt the terribleness of the first war—I call them the homogeniuses—this is not to say, as many do, that this group contributed only a kind of mystical emptiness, a wasteland feeling.

Very much to the contrary. As I watched things in the thirties, I was amazed to see the practical effect of the philosophy of mysticism we discussed years before and were told was completely impractical. Theoretical.

They used to say it was mysticism but events proved that, as in other times, people were incorrectly interpreting "mysticism." Mysticism has always denoted a larger personality, with more senses than the average. Today's mysticism becomes tomorrow's reality. I remember the time when Ibsen appeared as almost a mystic to people because he tackled the breaking of woman's chains.

Well, after the first World War some of the homogeniuses turned to what the newspapers insanely pooh-poohed as phony-baloney cultism, when it actually was a reaching out for a sense of the wholeness of the human being. Like Mark Tobey, Mark embraced Bahai, and so did I because this is a concept of the universality of man, God, nature—a refreshment of Judaism and Christianity combined. Tobey said he learned from Bahai to get out of the way and let simple profound nature take over his work.

Lo and behold, beginning in the thirties more people began to appreciate that the homogeniuses had something with their phony-baloney. I don't mind quoting Maxwell Bodenheim again on this because his tragedy came not from lack of deep insight but from inability to apply it for himself. Anyway, before his death he pointed out how more and more people were finding Freudianism insufficient because it dissects and cross-indexes your palpitations when what you need is a sense of the Whole—synthesis, not analysis. Marxism infringes on freedom, which is imperative to the creative person. And Buddhism simply allows you to remove yourself from the world, rather than to act upon it.

So Buddhism is N.G., also Freud, also Marx. Likewise trying to build a bridge to life entirely of instinctive sex, drink, or by the route of the marijuana smokers whom we called "vipers." I was watching with great interest during the thirties, the small beginnings of a recognition that "mysticism" was becoming reality for those who shape the world thought.

Bahai, partly yes. Some part of Zen Buddhism. But for me and others, almost as much the methods and concepts of Gurdjieff. Who is Gurdjieff? A few years more, nobody will need to ask. His staff brought him to me the first time in the early twenties, a trip from Europe financed by Lady Rothermere of England, but he came often again in later years. About twelve of them came that first time, brought to my little place by Muriel Draper and a whole group of other people.

Gurdjieff was a Russian, from Georgia, but he came in, he looked like a Turk. Big mustache, great black eyes. He had a place later in Fontainbleu, France, to which all kinds of great people—engineers, scientists, architects—migrated, to live around him and to take from him the wisdom of this method. Later on, Peter Brook, the director, couldn't shake himself free from fascination with Gurdjieff.

Anyway, as I say, he came in and the first thing he did was stare at me. That man was so clairvoyant, I discovered, so that when he looked at something he almost immediately knew it from top to bottom. So while he stared at me, those knowing him started asking him, "What kind of idiot is she?"

It turns out that he classified people by various kinds of idiocy. This is because most of us take time to go looking in the bank and take stock of our property, but few of us take time to figure out our personal faculties that are our inside property. The result is dissipation of energy inside, instead of energy put into action. It is "idiocy" to do this.

So Gurdjieff classified people as pernicious idiot, hopeless idiot, zigzag idiot, unique idiot. He said this stirs people up, makes them ask "why?," and that is the beginning of thinking. Well, when he was being asked to classify me—listen, there were people who claimed I was influenced because I was fascinated with the man, but through the years I always held to the way he answered about me. He said, "This woman is no idiot, she is what is called essence friend." How do you like that? He said in my essence I am a friend to the world.

But that is not why I am recalling Gurdjieff. It is because of his concepts. He wrote a book designed to be read three times—once aloud, once softly, then finally to yourself. In the book he pointed out that when you do not take that time to inventory and understand your inner properties you are leaving work unfinished.

Such unfinished work is a delicate poison, he said, a cancer you can watch being built. It's like an accumulation of dirt. And how can you expect people to sort out and cleanse their spiritual properties when some do not even take enough time to sit on the toilet and clean their stomachs?

He said what's needed is a clear awakening to the way of stepping into your whole being. There are three centers: the heart, the matter upstairs, the brain, and then the machine in which they are housed. So many people use the brain matter when they should use the heart, he said, and use the heart when they should use the machine. So many people are either all mental or all physical. They use and administer to only one center, the others go unused and uncared for, and the result is breakdown, neurosis, insanity.

Of course, Gurdjieff said, it takes real knowledge to use all the centers, it takes perfect harmony, first with yourself. The best time to start this is in childhood, when little vistas are formed from smell, hearing, taste, feel, and that is why whole families were sometimes going to stay at Gurdjieff's Fontainbleu place.

Well, I watched him operate on this thesis.

By working with all his centers—he even called eating "feasting" because eating was a ritual to serve one center, not just a stomach-stuffing—he was able to accomplish things quickly that take most people many hours or many days. He would go sit in the Childs Restaurant that used to be on Columbus Circle here in New York. And there, amid the clatter of dishes, with some black coffee and lemon, he would finish between seven o'clock and noon enough writing to occupy fifteen people he had working for him.

Another thing was that because he was using and taking proper care of all his centers, four hours sleep was sufficient. His energy was so well-used that, with all his centers at rest, this was all he needed. In bed at three and by seven in the morning he was up and out, to write again or go for a walk if he didn't write. But he made the big point that you can't have that thorough sleep with all your centers, if you've left something unfinished, because anything you have on hand must have its proper stage completed or it makes a weight, it tires you. Feeling that you have completed a thing or a logical part of it is important because it is going on to the next task that gives you energy.

Of course he didn't let me off the hook, this Gurdjieff. When he told me I was essence friend and I answered eagerly that yes, I like to share whatever it is I have, especially the happiness I brought from my childhood in nature, he told me, "But you're not sharing, you're just throwing it out and sometimes it's used but sometimes it's not.

"You must learn to manipulate it," he told me, "Give them laughter and sunshine, that's fine, you have enough in you to throw around. But other things, wait until people come to you and seek, only then give."

I am recalling all this about Gurdjieff because many of us felt the fantastic outpouring of new energy, new spirit in the thirties was a manifestation of the Gurdjieff ideas. If only people realized it, then it could have been consciously sustained.

When he came to see me in the late forties for what proved to be the last time, he really was scheduled to return and establish a center in America but he said to me, "Perhaps not. Perhaps I will go too far to return."

He was right. He died aged, about a hundred. Before he did, there came to him a couple of students from Asia who said, "Master, your knowledge is wonderful, but we're not going to believe it until you teach us and the world how to control death—not to let it come and take a person away when they're interested in doing things. When and if you succeed in doing that, then we'll believe everything you know." His answer was to kiss their foreheads and say, "All right, my boys, the task of controlling death is already begun, because your questioning the inevitability of death is the beginning. Science will soon bring a time when a life span of 150 years will be nothing, but by your questioning you have already taken the first step toward the task of making such longevity more than just a thing of vegetable existence."

I feel very fortunate in having met a sage like that in this world. Sometimes wisdom comes in strange or unruly packages. Sometimes we learn even from those who are failures in the world's eyes but have great integrity within themselves.

Such a one was the man who came to work for me during the Depression. You know, anybody who worked for me stayed with me for years. I had my cook for 16 years, and one cleaning woman for 10 years, and if one of them would leave because of some personal problem or because they would go on to success artistically, it would be almost tragic for me, because I was lost.

Well my cleaning woman had to leave me, she had to go home to Jamaica in the West Indies where her mother was dying, so this time I called the Salvation Army. They sent me a middle-aged, dried-up, fidgety person who rushed around all over the place to look it over, then told me how capable he is, he cleans very well and all that.

I stood there, watching him, and then I asked, "Have you got any references?"

He said, "No, I lost everything. I have nothing. Nothing." As he was saying that, I had a good look at him, at the texture of his skin and all, and I thought, this man must have seen better days. I could see that he must really have suffered some tragic losses. I was thinking this about him when, all of a sudden, his bitter, sour face cracked into a smile, and he said, "But I've got this."

He put his hand in his pocket and took out a three-quarter-yard long string, thick with keys. What was this?

"This is entrusted to me by the owners of a big building on Broadway, where I run the elevators every Sunday," he said. I thought to myself, well this is good, this is a true reference, if they trust him with all those keys, then I can trust him with mine.

"Oh," he said, "you don't know how well I know thieves when I see them." And he began to give me a whole lecture on the psychology of thieves. How they come sneaking around but how he always sees them, he always notes them, they can't sneak around him.

I thought, "Oh, oh, he's upset about thievery, what is this?" But anyway I told him he had a very good reference. I gave him my keys and showed him what he had to do. Part of it was the room where I had exhibitions, changed every three weeks; I told him that a young artist would be coming in each time to take down the pictures then hanging and putting up new ones.

The man said, "But what if he runs away with those pictures?" Look,

I said, this young artist is like my son. But try as I might, I couldn't seem to convince the man. Finally I said, "Look, don't you worry about that. You clean up the place, you go away, and every Saturday I will meet you and pay you."

He kept at it. "Oh," he said, "you've got to watch out for things." Again he went on about the risk of the pictures being taken, and I had to end the conversation by telling him that was something for me to worry about, not him.

That man turned out to be the most conscientious cleaner. He did things he didn't have to do, taking phone messages and all. But invariably, each time my young artist would come to change the paintings, the man would almost foam at the mouth and threaten to call the police.

So one night I came to Stefansson and the crowd, they were sitting there, and I was commenting about it, saying this man must have a sickness, he must have been robbed himself or something that gave him this complex about people stealing. Well many of the others jumped on me for keeping him, they said the man himself must be a thief, only a thief would think so of other people. My answer was no, I could swear this man was honest and conscientious, that it must be a psychological thing with him.

Well the following Saturday, the place was spick and span, I walked in, he was ready for his wages but he had a big package under his arm, wrapped in newspaper. And listen, if that man had been rehearsed to play a thief he couldn't have done it better on stage. He moved backwards with the package held behind him, talking while he moved.

For instance, he picked up a little nail and said, "You don't need this little nail," still moving backwards. And I, leaning against the knob of the door, smoking and watching this man, a torment came to me. How am I going to let this man out with the package, yet how am I going to question him? I felt it would shake his sensitivity to question him, but I certainly did not intend to let him out with that package. The conflict was so strong in me that I just stood there and let him flit, he was flittering around but constantly backwards.

Finally, after a long time—I smoked a whole cigarette, slowly—I thought well, I've got to do it. So, nonchalantly, smilingly, I said, "What have you got in that package?" Whereupon that crack of a smile came into his face, and he said, "Dust."

I said, "Dust? With all these cans around, you have to carry out dust?" He began to lecture me about dust—that it's just like a thief. Dust steals into your soup, steals into your things, it's better that you get it collected and carry it out.

More torment for me. He says it's dust in the package, but can I believe that? I don't want to hurt the poor man, how am I going to ask him to show me that it's dust, when that will mean I suspect him? Well, again I tried to fix my position in a very calm way and said, very smilingly, "Let me see."

Whereupon he put down the package, saying, "Yes, dust is the biggest thief yet," and he began to unwrap and—lo and behold—dust!

I was so moved by the simplicity of this man's honesty. All the twists that some people would make of their suspicions, that this man must be a thief, when his twist was the simplicity of stubbornly continuing to emphasize honesty, after what I could only imagine had been terrible hurts and losses brought by other people's dishonesty. While he rewrapped the package he continued to talk about how dust would steal, and not for one second did he seem to think I had suspected him.

I was so moved that I had tears in my eyes. I thought to myself, dust does travel, and I felt like a thief. I, who had the thought in my head that he might be carrying something of value from my place, I felt like the thief.

He stayed on the job until, finally, one day the artist I had in charge of the paintings had to call the police and have the poor man taken to the hospital because he was getting so violent about the pictures being taken down. I learned that he had developed some sort of business venture that he'd been cheated out of. He had been cheated by life and society, and his nature was such that he accumulated these hurts instead of doing battle with them, and ended up cracked. But still true. Cracked but true.

Of course we all know the most difficult thing of all is to remain true either in great setback or amid great success. I was taking issue with Max Bodenheim that he put disloyalty at the door of people who happened to win recognition and then left the Village, just because they left. Success is not disloyalty except when it misshapes the heart. Like Bodenheim accused Fannie Hurst of turning cold and haughty when the fact is she and certain others always retained a sense of their beginnings in their spirit, never tried to suggest that the Village where they began was really beneath them now.

Fanny used to come very often to my place with Stefansson, and once I said to her, "I've got someone you absolutely must meet." That someone was Mary Sachs who was a marvelous story. Began as a poor, neglected nobody in Harrisburg, Pennsylvania, went to work in this little department store and had such a fantastic spirit she soon ended up running her own store, like a Parisian showplace, right across from the State Capitol. The thing with Hurst was that I discovered, when Mary Sachs was ready to open her great store, she had gone to a movie to clear her head and the movie was the Hurst story with the hand in it of the Jewish violinist—*Humoresque*. And Mary Sachs had made her opening the talk of the town by bringing in the music of that movie, and involving all the children from the local institutions, but now it was years later and she never had met Hurst.

It happened I was sailing for that trip to Mexico at the time, but Fanny said, "Marie, when you get back, I want you to come up for dinner with me and bring that Mary Sachs." Well when I returned, I did just that. Mary Sachs curled up on Fanny's divan and told her story from seven o'clock to two in the morning, and when I was getting home, the telephone in the hall already was ringing, it was Fanny calling to pour out to me her delight. She still had all her zest.

I want to recall another who, by ordinary standards was a failure, but who all his life bespoke such a sense for beauty that in his own peculiar way he may have been almost as much a sage as Gurdjieff— and in more glorious ways than Hurst could put ecstasy into words. That was Sadakichi Hartmann, who continued to come in occasionally in the thirties, and even once later. Like Gurdjieff, he too was one of those who almost forgot to die. Imagine, he was a man who got admiring words from Walt Whitman.

I said that Sadakichi was among those at the head of the group that first convinced me to start up in the Village. From all the sponging he did on me through the years after that, I would be entitled to call him names. Some have written stories about him like that: parasite, faker, great deceiver. But to do that would be to judge by only the one side of human nature, by one shadow, when most people are made up of several shadows—of constant conflict between the rigid and cruel side, and the beautiful, tender and loving side.

How could you call names at a man who, in memory of the Japanese girl who died giving him life after she had it with his German father, could write a beautiful, tender poem about her:

A woman's death created me.
Rest with my thanks,
Rest softly under the hills of Kobe;
While wind and birds sing everlasting
Funeral rites to thee, my mother.

I think best of Sadakichi from the time he came to sit over a bottle of wine with me, my Mother, and Leonard Abbott. As I said, Sadakichi looked like a long, thin stick with a cape around it. Naturally, Sadakichi wanted something.

I told Leonard, "Sadakichi wants the use of your little summer house in Westfield, New Jersey."

"What?" said Leonard. "In the winter cold?"

Sadakichi said, "Ah, Madonna will love it. It has a fireplace, doesn't it? Madonna always loves to live like this." Madonna was then Sadakichi's wife—actually more people were calling her "Dreamy," that was more her real name, but Sadakichi called her "Madonna."

Anyway he bothered so much that he got the keys to the house. Madonna was arriving the next day and I was very anxious to talk to her, to get from her whether she really wanted to live in a place with the nearest neighbor two miles away.

Here came this tall, phantom-like woman, big with child. And these little children with her, running after him, calling him Kichi. These magnificent-looking little children running, and she with child, a tall phantom-like woman. I said,

"Madonna, Sadakichi tells me you won't mind living in a place where all the pipes are shut down, no heat or anything."

She said, "He knows. There is snow, I can make water from the snow. I will love it." Many women were that way about Sadakichi.

All right, so we called a taxi and we put in the children and I bought a big basket of provisions and we all went out to Westfield. Cold, and imagine, she was about to give birth to a baby but she said she didn't need a doctor, she didn't need anybody. We left her there, he came too because he was living in a hotel in town, he left her there with the children and the baby coming.

Well, once settled out there, Sadakichi reported to me that the children were like little rabbits running in the snow. They were all happy. But one night, late, he came to me and said, "Madonna is about to give birth to her baby." I just shuddered, has she got a doctor? He said, "No, she doesn't need one."

This Polly Holladay who used to have a place in the Village was an old friend, Sadakichi knew her when she was a girl, so I called Polly and said, "Look, you better get out to New Jersey, your friend Dreamy is giving birth tonight alone there, in the cold, without a doctor near." Polly trekked out there in the snow and the storm and when she knocked at the door, Madonna said, "Who's there?"

"This is Polly Holladay."

Madonna came down, opened the door and said, "Thanks but I don't need you, go away," and there was nothing Polly could do but go away.

Next thing I knew, Sadakichi and Madonna were coming in and I saw the little baby, looking like an old Japanese. Dreamy was happy, everything was wonderful. But that summer Marigold, one of the other children who was then seven, fell from a swing, fell off and hit her head and died of spinal meningitis.

Sadakichi became absolutely miserable. He loved that child so. He had asthma and every time he convalesced he used to go out there and take walks with Marigold, have conversations with her. He said to me, "I can't live without her, it's impossible. Of all the children I loved her. I'll invent a religion that will give me hopes of seeing her again."

I said no, he'd done enough to religion. Once, he wrote a book saying Jesus was in love with Mary Magdalene. "You write a little book of all the conversations you had with her," I told him. Fine. He's going to write the most beautiful little book, with her picture on the cover. Nothing was said anymore. He went to California to see how he could make the necessary money to publish such a book.

That following winter, I was in my place one night when a man walked in and asked if I was Romany Marie.

Yes.

He said, "I'm a director of Famous Players for Douglas Fairbanks. You know Sadakichi Hartmann, you're a friend of his, so you ought to know that if we can find him we'll probably shoot him." I said, what?

He said, "Yes, we'd like to shoot him because he really misled us, really put one over on us. We invested $50,000 around him and he didn't come through and ended up costing us $250,000."

He went on to spin the whole story.

"One night I walked into a joint in Hollywood," he said, "and there is this man in a corner who looks like a Chinese prince. I went over to him and I said, 'My God, a Chinese prince. Come with me to Fairbanks, you're just the man we need for the court magician in the *Thief of Baghdad*.'"

This director continued that Fairbanks found Sadakichi correct for the role even without any makeup, offered him $400 a week plus a case of whiskey a month, and Sadakichi consented. But after they had done a lot of costuming and shooting and everything, one morning Sadakichi didn't appear.

I said, "Well, from what I know of Sadakichi, early in the morning he always had an attack of asthma. He always has been very embarrassed, and too proud to tell anybody about it."

To that, the director said I shouldn't suggest to him that Sadakichi's attacks went on for weeks, because that's how long Sadakichi hid out. All the scenes had to be rephotographed with a different actor, and when the newspapers finally located him, Sadakichi said, "The reason I didn't continue is because Fairbanks sent me rotten whiskey."

So, the director told me, that's why they'd like to shoot him.

I said, "My dear man, do you know what he was really doing while you read his excuse in the papers? He was panting for breath, he was nearly dying. Many is the time we engaged him to come read here in the place and he did the same thing. Gave the excuse that he had to go open the gas for Madonna who had just moved to Philadelphia, when in fact he would telephone me secretly, 'Come quick, I'm dying, bring me a little bottle of whiskey, I'm dying,' and I'd go to him and find him sitting on the edge of his bed, wheezing and gasping with a death mask look on his face."

The director said to me, "Oh, that's his act. You must be in love with him to believe that."

Well as far as I'm concerned, the proof of the pudding was that, the next thing, I received in the mail a most handsome little book from Sadakichi, with Marigold's picture on the cover, as he'd planned. He published about 500 copies, just for select friends. It had some lovely things in it, inspired by that dead child.

> Tell me autumn night,
> What is perturbing my mind?
> Is it that I wait
> For one who does not come,
> Or is it the moan of the wind?

He'd worked just long enough to get the sum of money he needed for the book, then quit because he couldn't go on, he was too sick a man for that kind of movie work, but his Japanese trickery made him invent a crazy, foolish reason why.

This is not to suggest that Sadakichi was not difficult. He was a kleptomaniac. He was very proud that he could take things in the speediest way, in the presence of other people, and nobody would know. But he would take only from friends and send the things to other friends.

One day I missed a very beautiful French pin, I couldn't find it anywhere. A year passed. One day Sadakichi walked in and said, "Madam, these are for you, in return for that French pin," and he gave me a beautiful pair of earrings. They were Madonna's, he'd sent my pin to Madonna, and she sent the earrings for the pin.

Another time he came to tell me delightedly that a woman sculptor whom he called his lady friend, living on Washington Square South, was doing his bust. He was happy with the arrangement because she was feeding him and taking care of him, and he still had plenty of time to write, he was then working on a sequel to his book, *Is Peace a Permanent Dream?*

But after a few weeks he came to say they have had a falling out, the bust was almost finished but she didn't want him around anymore. All the while that he was reporting this to me, he was calling on his German efficiency to figure out how he could obtain that bust because he regarded it as his rightful property.

"I'm looking for a Big Six," he told me, "six tall young men who can join me in going to her ground floor studio to retrieve that bust and assure it an appropriate fate." And he did exactly that, found six fellows who were amused by the idea, and they sneaked the bust out while the sculptress was sleeping.

What I didn't learn until later was that he then went with the bust to the downstairs Grill Room of the old Brevoort Hotel, put the bust on the table and ordered food and drink for two while he held conversation with the bust as though it was a live companion. When he was finished, he got up, bowed, then went to the cashier's cage and said, "That gentleman over there will pay." Before the cashier had a real chance to look Sadakichi was gone. He came to my place and said, "Madame, do you wish to have a bust of Sadakichi Hartmann?"

Sure, I said.

He said, "Go to the Brevoort and ask for it." I did, and I had to pay the check. But it was a good bust, I wish I knew what happened to it.

Actually, the people he insulted were only those he felt didn't understand his books. Charles Byington, who retired from being a big cheese executive, a cheese king, to take up photography in the Village, was one of these. Byington loved Hartmann's books and tried to collect them; he would send Sadakichi whole big cheeses for the books, besides paying a good price for them. But, alas, he didn't click with Sadakichi. Once, when Byington wrote to him that he was lacking just one book in his collection, Sadakichi wrote back and said, "Since when does a cheese man know anything about books? Send $20 in advance."

Anyway, the final thing about Sadakichi is that I discovered his very first wife was a wonderful woman because one day she came into my place—looking quite badly, quite emaciated—and said, "Perhaps you would like to know that I am Mrs. Sadakichi Hartmann."

I said, "What? Which one?"

She said, "I'm the first one, the one that had two sons with him and two daughters." She had with her an old handbag, and from it she produced this yellow piece of paper. It was their marriage license.

"I came to tell you he is very ill out in California," she said. This was at least thirty, forty years after he'd left her with little children to bring up herself, so I said, "Why are you worrying?"

"Ah," she said, "I had great appreciation for him, he was a little bit monster but a great deal a lover and a genius, and now he shouldn't be allowed to suffer." I asked her, what about herself?

"Well, he told me I'm not worth a farting," she said. "The fact is, I used to be a poet myself."

I told her, "Lift your head, the sun shines for you as well as for him. He would respect you only if you believe that you are worthy of his love, else he would not have loved you."

When she left, she was standing straight and erect. Then I recall that the last time I saw him he told me that he had two daughters by still another wife, beautiful Japanese girls, and that he dearly loved one of them, has visited her once in a while. If he really was dying he would go to die in the home of this girl in Florida, to see her one last time. He said, "I will travel half-dead if necessary, but I will die at her threshold."

Only a few weeks later, I heard he had done it. He came all the way from California to her, and as he got through her door, he died. It was in 1944.

That man left a strange feeling with the people he left behind. A good feeling, I think, in spite of everything. In the one book that was done of him where there was appreciation, Gene Fowler wrote it about Sadakichi and John Barrymore and W.C. Fields, and the painter John Decker whom I also had in the old days; Sadakichi was credited with courage. But even that book didn't credit his asthma as the real thing when he ran out on Douglas Fairbanks.

Well, I think different. He is appropriate to this chapter because he had what I imagine Walt Whitman would have said was a multitude of personalities. From several of them there were things to learn about beauty.

Depressions, wars, fakeries, times of tired spirit which are worse than tired blood—everything is inclusive, like additions that can be made to a central line in a painting. Only what belongs stays, invasions and discords fall away if you take the time to clean out the scene occasionally, like you clean out a room. Clean away the superfluities in the nature of a man like Sadakichi and treasure what adds to life's juices. If you are not interested enough to investigate the various shadows of such people, then leave them alone.

11. "DR." MARCHAND

Only a woman capable of taking at face value Sadakichi Hartmann's outrageous alibis could have remained for more than 40 years in love with Arnold Damon Marchand and staunchly respectful of his capacities as a chiropractor and inventor. At least that was the contention of some of Marie's relatives and many of her devotees.

They saw Marchand as a misogynistic faker. They conceded he could intrigue uptowners but they said he irritated many of Marie's regular followers. Certainly, his peccadilloes accentuated Marie's chronic need for having to meet the landlord at the door.

Marchand's regular write-off of explorer Stefansson, as an iceman "really named William Stevens", was only one of a myriad of notches in his verbal gun. Once, when two out-of-towners arrived with greetings from painter Mark Tobey, Marie called, "Marchand, Marchand! Come meet some friends of Mark's." From the kitchen came Marchand's growling, "Who wants to meet friends of Mark Tobey?" This was followed by a crash as he exercised a favorite ploy and dropped a stack of dishes on the floor. Marie, as was her wont, laughingly shouted in that husky voice of hers, "Save the pieces!" winning further admiration for herself but not especially repairing Marchand's public relations.

But he had his advocates among some of the regulars who came in the late thirties and early forties to Marie's places, on Eighth Street, Thirteenth Street, and then at two successive locations on Grove Street. They insisted that Marchand showed a considerable, if selective, warmth. They also envied his admirable readiness to shoot at idols as he fired salvos from his favorite spot, a wicker chair with a great, half-moon back, in the lee of which he looked like Mark Twain after a bad review.

Eschewing Marie's reading of coffee-grounds, Marchand used palmistry to bite the hands of patrons he thought needed some come-down. To ebullient author-playwright William Saroyan, Marchand said after fingering the Armenian palm, "You're full of cheese. You charge up to a subject but the minute you get really close to it, you back away." Saroyan is reputed to have said delightedly, "Yes! Other people just tell me how good I am, you're the first non-critic ever to tell me the truth."

On another occasion, Marchand studied the palm of one of New York's most sought-after psychiatrists. "You, sir, are a fraud because you are mastering other people's lives in order to try to master your own," Marchand rumbled. "You should try the nut house."

His palmistries, like Marie's coffee-cup readings, were advertised as a free amusement but Marchand crossed Marie by announcing to some whom he disliked that he could offer only a one-dollar "casual reading" or a five-dollar "deep reading"; these who opted for the short version were told, "You're practically finished." For patrons to whom he had an especially negative reaction, he flamboyantly went through a ritual of hauling out the garbage before coming to read their palms.

Marchand's linguistic side had made his own brand of phonetics one of his passions. To this Marie yielded by allowing him to prepare her menus phonetically. These proclaimed "ate kyndz Terkish kawfee," "rowsst beef" and "stood proons," and failed to unnerve regulars only because they knew Marie's cuisine so well. In a 1935 letter which he typed for Marie to one of her nephews, on the stationery of the Eighth Street version of the Romany Marie Tavern ("in the famous Della Robbia Room—a center for all arts and artists"), Marchand wrote,

"Luv to Cillya and Popa, am sure thay r boath prowd ov yewoo. Reed d inklowzd menyoo end yew wil reelyz d sick-nee-fee-cans uv simp lee feyd spelink, whair evree sil lahbl haz a meen ink oar a purfikt dis torshn end yet fonetical lee core rect. Veree mutch apreesheeayshn frum unkl Da non."

In each of her places, Marie resignedly condoned Marchand's use of cellar-space or an extra room as a repository for his constantly growing accumulation of health books and treatises, and paraphernalia and materials for his endless chemical experiments. The result was a colossal shambles that, after the start of World War II, brought some official suspicion that Marie's Grove Street basement housed an enemy demolition unit.

Some of Marchand's inventions were not lacking in breakthrough quality. Around 1927, he described an idea for a central transportation building that would provide travel information and tickets to any place in the world by any mode of travel. He also worked on formulas for an instant coffee, a shaving cream to do away with razors, and a solution to prevent runs in hosiery. But somehow they all ended up merely enlivening Marie's existence. In 1940, to promote an idea for a vitamin coffee, Marchand erected across the street from Marie's restaurant a sign that was bigger than Marie's own modest, lantern-shaped symbol, and that took the play away from it. "Vita Coffee Co. of America," the sign said. That's all there was to the business, just the sign.

His training in midwestern schools of chiropracty and osteopathy gave Marchand some right to use the title of "Doctor," but his ill-fated venture up on Broadway was his only stab at formal practice.

Yet Marie persisted in her sublime faith in his wisdom on health matters. In the end, it was his stubborn avoidance of medical attention for a prostate gland condition that led Marie in 1946 to close her Grove Street restaurant, and to devote three years to nursing him in a nearby basement apartment.

"Dr. Arnold D. Marchand, beloved husband of the famous Romany Marie, died Dec. 23 at 21 Grove Street, after an illness of six years," the *Village Voice* reported with solemn dignity in 1949. "Born in 1874, he was a great humanitarian, gave generously to many worthy causes. Author of *Language is Power*, he was a liberal and a philosopher, and one of the Village's most popular and picturesque citizens."

A few days after his death, Marie knocked at the door of the Central Park West apartment occupied by her friend, Joe Julian, a well-known radio actor. When Julian's wife answered, Marie said, "I came for a favor. Do you have a can opener?"

Mrs. Julian turned but then did a double take. "Marie—a can opener?"

"Yes, yes," Marie said, holding up a can. "I've got Marchand in here and I've got to go scatter him." Once suitably equipped, she went off into the park to dispose of Marchand's ashes along the bridle path, where he had asked they be deposited because horses are nobler than people.

───────────────────

Marie:

Success in the conventional way is often a terrible disruption. For some people, failure in the conventional sense is something they can live with more productively than success. What the world sees as failure is often for such people a real success. I have often thought that some of the young people we have seen coming up since the second World War, who are momentarily without stars, without dreams, they were called beatniks but perhaps they should be called anti-successors because they found comfort in their maladjustment.

When you come down to it, it's the old story. I had coming to the place in 1940 a young commercial artist who was already handling some of the biggest products in America. Advertising artist. But he wasn't happy with this success, this George. He felt shame. We were talking long hours about how he could fit into his success the things of value in his work which he felt he had abandoned. Since the war, little by little, he began injecting into his commercial work the elements of his real art. He was making a marriage in his work.

The thing many people didn't understand about Marchand was that he had no taste for such a balance. No patience. He was so consistent in his determination not to go in conventional ways that he fought it until the end of his life. And that's why I loved him, because he did it in action.

Any invention of his that had a tendency to be taken up by somebody and developed for the market, he immediately let it go and started another one. He did this without philosophizing about it. When some railroad people came to see him about a formula for instant coffee, he ran away from them. He was happiest when he was developing. Of course, this made for some peculiar occasions.

Ivan Black, who was so responsible for bringing the big name to Café Society Downtown and Café Society Uptown when they were among New York's most popular night places, Ivan came in one time with a beautiful girl. A black-haired model. Beautiful. And she wanted Marchand to read her palm. "Tell my fortune," she said. Well this "fortune" business didn't click with Marchand.

"You're happy the way you are, aren't you?" he told her. "You don't want to meet me." And he walked off. The girl said to Ivan, "Well! He is different, isn't he?"

In a little while, Marchand returned to them carrying a bowl in which he had one of his solutions. "You are a very beautiful girl," he said to her. "I like the way you look, so I'm going to do something for you. Please take your stockings off."

Well, the girl looked at Ivan, and Ivan looked back at her and said, "If Dr. Marchand says take your stockings off, take them off."

Marchand explained, "I have a reason. I have a formula here that will so fix your stockings that never again will there be a run in them." He rolled up the stockings and put them into the bowl. As Ivan and the girl watched, the stockings dissolved into liquid. Ach! Marchand said. He had made the stuff a little too strong again. He went off to his laboratory in the cellar and in a few minutes he came back with some salve, Ivan should try a little on his beard to see that Marchand didn't make all his chemicals too strong. It was Marchand's concoction for rubbing off the beard, you wouldn't need ever to use a razor.

Naturally, Ivan said Marchand should first give a demonstration, so Marchand put a little on his own arm. Well, he had to rush over to St. Vincent's Hospital for emergency treatment for a chemical burn. Marchand had used too much sulphur.

The thing is, how many inventors throughout history did not have some such bizarre experiences? And Marchand was always ready to test his things on himself. Always.

If he was often sarcastic to people, well even those whom he made bitter admitted to me that he usually did it in style, so that some considered it almost an honor to be insulted by Marchand. People who remember his breaking dishes would have to know that, as he once said to me, "If I didn't do this, I might break someone's head. Which is better?" Of course, the reason for his sarcasm was that, underneath, he didn't want to be with people. It was I who drew him into contacts with people. His happiness was when the place was closed and we two had our own simple, little world.

Otherwise, he was one of those people who are at their best with children and with animals. They felt him. I'll never forget one of those summers we spent in Gloucester, Massachusetts, a whole group of us went to the town where we saw a man with a little monkey. The man played some sort of a drum, while the monkey ran about in a little apron, jumping up to each person's pocket in search of a coin. Some people reacted skittishly, others laughed. And the little monkey was working so hard.

Marchand and I stood on the outskirts. The monkey spotted him and fought his way through. And instead of going to Marchand's pocket, the monkey went straight up to his face and embraced him, the monkey had tears running. I am convinced the animal felt that Marchand would have a sympathy for him, instead of laughing or showing nervousness, and it was so. To those who tell me "pooh pooh" on this, my answer is have you ever noticed how animals—yes, and children—instinctively take to some people, and not to others? It is an intuition.

It worked that way as I have described in the great immigration days on Ellis Island, when Marchand worked there as an interpreter. Marchand, and also Fiorello LaGuardia who had the next desk, both of them always with a regular court around them of tired, dirty and miserable children from all over the world.

Marchand, himself, came from a family that produced many children without any real rhyme or reason and were fighting and scrapping all their lives. Marchand left when he was a youngster, went into the cavalry, then traveled all over the world, learned all those languages. He was always traveling. In later years, his traveling was from day to day. He didn't care to accumulate wealth, he accumulated knowledge, he accumulated love for children and other honest, uncontrived things.

It's true that he also accumulated all kinds of junk, but this became the focus of one way in which Marchand showed he could use his magic of intuition on older people when it was necessary.

Between his chemicals, and his books on languages and anatomy and chiropractic and all that, he accumulated things fantastically. At times when I didn't know what to do anymore—so many things in the way I could hardly find my way to bed—and I threw things out, he would go and bring them back.

Understanding his longings, I never reprimanded him. But for one ten-year period, to be able to handle it, I rented for him at ten dollars a month a separate little basement where his entire collection could be.

We all called it "the Garbage Can." Take it to the garbage can. That little place was so stuffed that you could hardly walk into it. When he needed something that was in there, it was often easier to go out and buy it, rather than try to find it. But it was working fine until they decided to tear down the place where the Garbage Can was located, and I couldn't find another place anywhere.

I sat down quietly with Marchand and said, "What's the use of keeping so many of these things? Let's give most of them away." He almost wept, but finally he agreed with the understanding that he would pick out certain things to be saved. Well, he picked out a truckful—and when the Salvation Army came to look at the remainder, they wouldn't take them. They didn't mean to the Salvation Army, even, what they meant to Marchand.

The upshot was all the things ended up in the basement of my Grove Street place, including the laboratory table where he stood working, in a white apron, certain hours of every day. It was already wartime, and I thought my God, he'll be accused of making bombs or something. He had already had one small explosion while working on his beard-remover cream.

Things came to a peak when our landlord came to say he had a board of health order that basements must be clean. He went down to look at ours and was horrified; if we didn't clean it up, the restaurant could be condemned and also the whole building. Marchand promised but kept putting it off, putting it off. "I have only one more thing to finish," he would say. He was that much engrossed in his inventions, not so much to put them over but as the interest of an artist in his art.

Alas, this went on until one day an inspector did appear, and this is where I get to the point about Marchand's potential as a person of certain persuasive energy. I was all alone in the kitchen when the man walked in, looked around, then went into the little hall near the cellar stairs and said, "What have you got down there?"

Aiyyyy! I almost died. I said, "That's a basement." He said, "Can you show me down?" He was from the fire department, no less. I called down to Marchand who was there working, "Listen, there is a gentleman here from the fire department who wants to come down." I thought he'd be frightened, in the middle of that unbelievable mess, all those chemicals. Not Marchand. There he appeared, in his white apron, all flushed, he looked up and said with a big grin, "Let him come down."

I left them and walked into the kitchen. One hour passed, two hours, I thought, "My God, what are they doing down there?" But I didn't want to mix in, I felt it was Marchand's business to decide how to handle it, to give himself up if he had to.

Believe it or not, they were there four hours, four hours I didn't hear from them. Finally, up they both came, both of them very elated. The inspector came to me, "Where did you get this man? He's loaded with ideas, he's a wonder." I was astonished. It turned out the inspector chanced to be a fellow who was also interested in some of the things Marchand was doing and longed for the day when he, too, could tackle such things. He left praising Marchand, quite forgetting what he had come for. When the landlord heard about it, he thought it would prompt Marchand to take the big step, but the truth is it took another period of time to get the landlord to help me hire a truck and get the things removed. And it was pathetic to see Marchand when he watched his laboratory being broken up.

He showed an amazing strength of mind and will about those subjects that interested him. In the health field, he was in his own way learned about anatomy and medicine, he had compiled information about the many great physicians who through the years were critical of the practice of the medical sciences—not the sciences but the practice of them.

I cannot begin to name all the people, famous and not, whom I helped by sharing with them Marchand's knowledge of how to use pressures to relieve various painful conditions. I have relieved myself of headaches, I have stopped arthritic pains by use of the pressures Marchand taught me. He brought in the scientific way many of the same curatives that my mother had drawn from nature in an old-fashioned, folk-style way.

Look, instinctively what do you do when you've hit yourself against something? The first thing you do is put your hand to the point of pain and rub it. Well, the gypsies from whom my mother learned took that from instinct; they said if instinct commands this sort of response, then we'll go further and see how to expand it.

Mother was a healer. She used to cure what we today call tonsillitis. With just a little bit of ointment, she'd go for hours and hours gently massaging the tonsils from the outside, and do away with the irritation. Of course, other things went with this. She believed in putting on compresses, and she also believed, as I've said, in blossoms and herbs in oils and in alcohols. As she manipulated, she'd quietly voice a whole, long recitation. They weren't chants but they weren't prayers either, they were more like asking the bad elements to disappear. She'd say, "I came across you, I met you, and you told me you were carrying these superfluous weights, these pains. I am here to talk your pains away, to throw them to the wilderness where the air will take them, the wind will blow them and the dust will absorb them."

She would say this to herself, you saw her lips moving as she rubbed you. Secret talks to the elements. We'd always noted that she made a place quiet when she gave a treatment. I mentioned how in Romania, when that healing monk saw her at the bedside of a sick person, he would quietly walk away: If you have her, you don't need me.

So there was healing in the family, and when I married this man, Marchand, it was marriage to a man perpetuating such healing through science. Twenty-one things to do before you get up in the morning, using the sensitivity in the tips of your fingers: For 15 minutes before you even get out of bed, relax and sensitize the body, go over your head with the tips of your fingers, like a vibrator.

I think of the people who have come to me—painters, dancers, writers—to moan how they're suffering from a headache, and almost always with a name for it, migraine heading the list. And so many times, I've said, "Look, just for fun, before you get out of bed tomorrow morning, sensitize your head." And I'd show them how. Oh, no, they begin to tell me how many medicines they've taken. My answer is, listen, do you really want to get rid of that headache, or do you like the name of it too well, do you really prefer to keep it?

Occasionally, one of them would try. Sometimes they'd be ashamed to admit it, but finally I would hear them saying to somebody else, "Marie showed me what to do, and my headache's gone." And of course, so often, that other person would say, "Aw, poppycock, not for me, I've taken six aspireens today and my headache hasn't gone, so why should this help? I better take a stronger kind of aspireen."

Marchand minced no words in this kind of situation, and sometimes it helped. It certainly did around 1945 or so, when New York was the scene of a regular cleanup drive among restaurants. With the cook I had then, it so happened that things were clean enough to eat off the floor, but even good hotels were being fined, so when two board of health inspectors appeared, I was frantic. While they rolled up their sleeves and went to work opening cupboards and so forth, I went upstairs to Marchand who was already sick, and reported to him.

Next thing I knew, Marchand was looking down at them from the stairway. He was dressed in his long, black robe, and leaning on his cane. He looked like a baron. "I want to see those men who are going to hang us," he said. The shorter of the two men went over to Marchand and said, "All right Pop, you better go back up to bed."

Marchand leaned toward him, and then away in distaste. "How can you come here to see if my place is clean, when your mouth smells so bad from your stomach?" he asked the man. "Look here, I'm a sick man, and you don't get such a smell from me. Here, give me a paper and pencil and I'll write down what you need for that stomach."

The little inspector blinked. Apparently he knew he had a problem. He took the paper on which Marchand wrote down what he needed, called to his assistant, "Go easy there!" and ran off to the drugstore. When he came back, he called the other inspector, said, "Never mind," and they left. End of inspection.

Marchand's magic insight into health phenomena, except where it concerned himself, was such that I never would cross it. One of the greatest men of medicine I have met in my lifetime was Dr. William Seaman Bainbridge, but even him I would have passed up if he had not passed Marchand's test that to be a great doctor you must bring into your practice the wisdoms of being a good and honest person.

Dr. Bainbridge's grandmother, I believe it was, had been America's first woman medical practitioner, and he carried this seed. You could see it by the chestful of medals he'd gotten during wars. He was a consulting surgeon and gynecologist to 16 hospitals, traveled all over the world and had his treatises translated into many languages.

Our experience with him began around 1932, when I was showing signs not only of exhaustion but also of something going on in my system. Stefansson called me over one night and said, "Marie, I don't like the way you look these days. Something is happening to you." I confessed that my mother had already had a couple doctors look at me, they had laughed and said they thought I had signs of pregnancy. Stef said, "I'll give you an introduction to one of the greatest, Dr. Bainbridge, let him look you over."

I decided I would go, but Marchand would have a say-so before anything would be committed. I walked into Dr. Bainbridge's office, they introduced me as Romany Marie who ran Stefansson's private club, and I saw this tall, handsome well-built body of a blue-eyed man, with a modest, serene manner. After only a brief examination of my abdomen he told me there were indications of a tumor. He said, "If you were my kin, I would take you in the car to my hospital, the Murray Hill hospital, and operate on you immediately." It was no pregnancy; he was willing to bet it was a tumor the size of a grapefruit and he'd advise surgery as soon as possible.

Well, we were approaching the Christmas season. When I told him I couldn't even think of surgery until after the holidays, he said, "What? You mean to tell me you're on your feet, working?"

I said sure, for 18 hours out of each 24. I invited him to come see for himself. He could visit with Stefansson there, and Marchand would have a fit knowing I was hemorrhaging and all; yet seeing me doing the cooking and running up and down stairs, he said to Stef, "What is this phenomenal thing? How does she do it?"

Stefansson explained my open secret, that I'm just lucky enough to be so assimilated, so taken up with the people in the place, that I can momentarily stay ahead of my aches. Frequently, during the time up to Christmas, Dr. Bainbridge came to watch me, while Marchand had his own chance to size up Bainbridge. Marchand never had opposed other people going for surgery, where there was something to remove, to make room for the osteopath or the chiropractor to make later adjustments and to build the person up. Marchand's opposition was to the routine practitioner, and when he met Dr. Bainbridge and read some of his writings, it made him sit up. This really was a man. "All right, go," Marchand told me. If it had been some lesser doctor and I had gone, Marchand would have repudiated me.

So, on the day after Christmas, I said to Dr. Bainbridge, "The morning of New Year's, I shall be willing to go for the operation." His answer was, "I hate to say this to you but it'll be New Year's IF you hold out!" Naturally I laughed and told him I felt wonderful, the blood I was losing must be bad blood. That was how I interpreted my hemorrhages, and Marchand was with me on this.

Come New Year's Eve, Dr. Bainbridge was there in the place with his gracious wife and two sons, and they watched me. From five in the evening until five in the morning I didn't sit down, the place was packed. Then, around six o'clock in the morning, my dear, sweet, jolly, saint-like mother arrived, escorted by Holger Cahill, to have breakfast with me and to take me to the hospital.

At the hospital, Dr. Bainbridge greeted me with, "I saw what you did all last night. You get an hour's rest and then we take you right up." He introduced me to the house physician who said if I wished I could invite Marchand, as a doctor, to watch the operation along with others who would have a place there. So finally there I was, and they were all dressed in white, including Marchand, standing almost on top of each other to watch me go.

I said, "Dr. Bainbridge, you still don't know me too well. Really all you know is from a little history in your office and from what you've seen or Stefansson has told you. I think you ought to know a bit more about me before you put the knife in. It will be springtime soon, and I certainly don't want to leave when spring is coming, I've fallen a little bit in love with this world, so there are some things I'd like to tell you."

Go ahead, he said. So I continued, "You know, I'm somewhat psychic, and in recent weeks I've had some strange dreams."

Dr. Bainbridge smiled and said, "You know, Marie, when my house physician here brought you in, he confided that you will come through and be better than ever. You see, he's psychic too. So go ahead, I'm anxious to hear you."

So while I lie there, waiting for the anesthesia with Marchand and the doctors around, I said, "Dr. Bainbridge, you should know that it's been 40 years since I've had a vacation. I'll tell you a secret, I know my tissues are very tired. Very tired. Can they stand a knife? I wonder."

I went on to enumerate the things I'd done in the previous 20 years in a hard way—the moving, the struggling, the difficulties with people. I told him that while I thought by nature I was not a sick person, nature might take its course. That brought me to the dreams I'd been having.

I knew the feeling and the smell of the grave. I had dreamt of people writing to me from all over the world to say they saw me all dressed up, all moving, dressed in white.

"Dr. Bainbridge, my interpretation of these dreams is that I'm finishing up here," I remember I said. "Now, I'm not afraid of death. I don't think there really is such a thing, yet I'm not religious enough to think there is such a thing as a hereafter." He looked at me dismayed, all Catholic.

"No, I'm not religious enough to accept a hereafter," I said, "but I am religious enough to love life, and that means accepting a concept of death as a transformation, a part of the ring of nature. This I do not fear, certainly not as much as I fear human beings living amid misunderstanding and thoughtlessness."

My God, Bainbridge and the others listened so intently, I never had a more wonderful audience. I talked for 25 minutes. When I was finished with the final words, I said, "Okay, now go right ahead, I no longer have fear. Go to it! So long!"

Needless to say, my dear mother stood with her ear to the telephone every minute of the operation. When they brought me down, my first question was had they advised her, my second was how long—I found the operation had taken 3 hours—and the third thing was, I want a cigarette. The nurse shushed me because she knew Dr. Bainbridge did not approve of anybody smoking in his presence. Whereupon he said, "Bring down a package of cigarettes," and the poor nurse was astonished. He went on, "This lady is to get everything she wants to help her psychology, that's the way she'll be healed."

I said, "Look, please don't force me to do anything, I will handle my pain the way I know to do. Don't give me any injections and don't give me any sleeping pills, I will handle it all myself." The house physician smiled and popped his eyes.

Temporarily, they put me in a room with a big, fat Irish woman who was having breakfast, putting a lump of butter, two soft boiled eggs and a pitcher of cream into her cereal. It made me so ill that since then I never look at food like that without the memory. I said, "Please, take me to a room where I can have my cigarettes and be alone."

They did, and after a day or so Dr. Bainbridge noticed that a great many people, instead of going to the center, were coming to see me, and I had a regular crowd waiting. Including Bob Chanler who brought me a beautiful screen he'd painted, to put in front of my bed, and who shouted at the poor nurse, "Nobody should have a say over this woman!" That nurse hadn't slept soundly nights for over 20 years. She heard Dr. Bainbridge say, "Look at this one, no sleeping pills, she just makes up her mind to sleep and she sleeps." Well, needless to note, I'd wake up at one in the morning and take Isadora Duncan's life to read, also Glenway Wescott's *Grandmothers*.

So once Dr. Bainbridge came in and found me with tears in my eyes, from a scene I'd just read that reminded me of Isadora. When I told him it was Isadora Duncan that I regarded as one of the greatest women America produced, Dr. Bainbridge, a highly moral man said, "That woman? Who had children with this man, outside of wedlock?"

I said, "Dr. Bainbridge, who has a right to judge a great person? What do I care about your private life, as long as you're a great surgeon? Am I going to question how you live from day to day? This woman has brought such beauty and movement..."

I began to tell him about her dancing and all. He listened, and finally he said, "All right! When you're through with that book, I want to read it." And he changed his mind, separated her greatness from his morality.

Times, he'd come in to ask how I was, and I'd say I felt very demoralized, so many things to do and I had to lie and look at the ceiling. "Ah," he said, "I thought you'd be complaining about some pain." Ha, ha, my pain is in that corner over there, I said, I tell my pain what to do. He made me have a night and day nurse, so I taught them how to make Turkish coffee, I'd be lying there and the whole staff would be around me so I could read their cups. In short, my room became

Romany Marie's. And for six weeks, he wouldn't let me out, because he knew I wouldn't take any time to convalesce.

Naturally, I was worried about the money. In the end, as I feared, I was all paid up for the hospital room and the nurses and the side things but the important element—Dr. Bainbridge's fee—was not paid. Well, within a week after I was back at the place he telephoned to say, "I want you to prepare a real Romanian dinner, I'm bringing down a bunch of surgeons to meet you." But he didn't bring surgeons, he surprised me with the entire hospital staff I'd had anything to do with. At the end of the dinner he knocked for attention and said, "Now we'll have the grand march with the trophy," and he held up in a glass jar, preserved, the growth he'd removed from me.

The showmanship of the man! Later, he saved my mother at 79 for eight, nine more years of alert life after some young doctor had given up on her, because Dr. Bainbridge saw her potential vitality from the twinkle in her eye.

Marchand was with me in this feeling about Bainbridge. People who didn't really know Marchand expected he would have some kind of jealous tantrum, like the afternoon I remember when a group of my important people were coming for a cocktail tea and I had the place spic and span. Until, that is, for some reason I don't recall, Marchand went around and spilled on the floor the contents of every sugar bowl. The people arrived before there was time to clean it up, so I explained that the sugar was on the floor from a rehearsal for an evening entertainment.

Marchand had no such explosion where Dr. Bainbridge was concerned. Later he had his own chance to shine professionally. It was some years afterward, when my Mother passed on, I was grieving very deeply but I had to control my grief because the center was there, and I had to go on. But in my control of grief, it didn't go up into the sky. It went into my body, and something happened. One morning, as I bathed, I saw that one of my breasts was black with a shine, it had turned purplish black. Quickly I called Marchand.

"Good God, what is that? Black!"

I said I was going to dress quickly and go to Bainbridge. Marchand said, "By all means. Before I tackle it, before I give you any treatments, you go to Bainbridge." Well, Dr. Bainbridge found there was a growth, but it could be removed in his office without any major work. For ten days before the removal I should go home and treat it with Epsom salt compresses.

When I carried this news to Marchand, he said, "Very well, this is my time, now I'll tackle it." He examined me and he found a ligament in the back that had been stretched, he found some veins busted and there was a little hemorrhaging going on. He had to relieve the ligament, straighten it out so as to make the blood circulate properly. This he did, and within four days I noted that the discoloring was disappearing. Within six days it was all gone. I put my hand under my breast, there was no growth there.

This I had to show to Dr. Bainbridge. I went to him and said I hadn't waited the ten days because of the improvement. He said it was amazing that the discoloration was gone so quickly, but the growth still had to be removed. All right, I said, so he begins to look.

"Wait a minute. I don't find it," he said. "Where is it?"

"I don't know."

"It's gone," he said. "I can't believe it. What have you been doing?"

"Well, Dr. Bainbridge," I said, "I know that you are of the old school and probably don't approve of unorthodox practices. But you do know I have a husband who is versed in osteopathy, in chiropractic. With all due respect to you, I thought that anything that might help would be good, so I let Marchand give me his treatments." And I went on to explain what Marchand had done. Whereupon Dr. Bainbridge said, "I have no monopoly on things like this. I must have a real talk with your husband." Until then, he hadn't; it had been a matter of Marchand sizing up Bainbridge, not vice versa.

Well, they had this talk. He told Marchand he was going to add his influence toward having osteopaths admitted to practice in the medical hospitals provided they could pass exams for medical knowledge. Marchand was in seventh heaven. They became good friends, and when Marchand became ill, Bainbridge was the first man I called.

It was around 1943, 1944. That's when Marchand failed. Dr. Bainbridge wanted Marchand to come immediately to the hospital, to be operated on but Marchand, the stubborn zealot, he believed he could do away with enlargement of the prostate by shrinking it with manipulations. He thought he could do for himself what he did for the five cats in the place, he manipulated their spines and as a result they had beautiful coats of fur, they never were sick.

Bainbridge told him no, he would get into terrible trouble, but Marchand was so opposed that he wrote a paper saying, "My enemies will take me to the slaughter house, my friends will let me stay in bed," and he put it under his pillow. Everybody was jumping on me to get him to the operating table, but me—I carried out Marchand's wish.

For the next two years I managed both the nursing of him and keeping up with the center. It was an eventful time in the world, of course, and my people were coming through from all the allied capitals, all the battlefields, hungry to recapture the continuity, to test their belief that out of this latest terrible world emergency could come valuable shakeups to bring awakening and hope and activity to backward people.

One day there came in a little man with a German accent, a refugee, he looked around and asked, "Is this the intellectual table?" He had heard of it while being bombed in London. "They said if I came here, I could relax and meet some interesting people." He was a physicist who was brooding that even if Hitler was defeated, Hitlerism could come again.

Anyway, he sat down and Joe Robinson, who was an officer of the Explorers' Club, asked him all kinds of questions. After a few hours, the man came to me and asked if Robinson was a spy, back in Germany only spies asked so many questions. Both Joe and I explained to him about the spirit of free inquiry the man had missed for so long, and out of it came another spontaneous friendship.

But the carrying on of this, together with caring for Marchand, became hard because the people I put in charge of the work in the place found it difficult to handle with me gone so often. My cook at that time was a wonderful woman, a mulatto named Birdie, she was so devoted. She learned to do my chorba and other dishes, she announced her independence from Southern cooking. She wrote one-act plays and enacted every character herself, people would call her to come out of the kitchen to give them one of her plays. Once, when I was invited to help in a war benefit at the Seamen's Institute downtown, I dressed her as a gypsy and she did one of her plays like that. She looked marvelous, showed such spirit and love, when she spoke the last line of her play in

a great voice—"The winning of the war is at hand!"—everybody cheered
and applauded for the Brown Gypsy.

But she worried and cried over Marchand's illness. One night when
the place was packed, I was trying to divide my time between Marchand
in his room and a whole group in the place led by diseuse Ruth Draper,
I was suddenly told that Birdie had fainted. I rushed to her and as I
brought her around and she opened her eyes, she said, "What do they
want of me? I can't stand it. I am not Romany Marie."

That decided me. I was then at 49 Grove Street, almost next door to
some saloon-type place that occupied the house where Tom Paine died,
and was calling itself "Marie's Crisis"—how do you like that, especially
when I was having the crisis! I had to make a choice between all-
Marchand or all-center, so my decision was to close up. I thought if it
was correct that I had made the place, that the place hadn't made me,
then I could open a fresh one and resume the caravan as soon as
Marchand got well.

I passed around word that I needed a little apartment to move to,
and meantime all my friends helped in the tremendous task of packing
all the things of the place. With the war coming to an end, there was an
enormous shortage of housing all over New York, and I waited and
waited for an apartment to show itself. Nothing.

Then, one Friday morning, I saw in the *Daily News* a big headline
that a man who lived less than a block from us on Grove Street, where
he had been teaching music, had been found murdered. As Marchand
and I looked at the man's picture, we decided he looked familiar to us.
So, not thinking of anything except learning the story, I went over to
see the building superintendent.

She told me the poor man had been a fine chap, quiet and minded
his own business, a good musician who had pupils coming to his
basement studio for piano lessons. The day before had been his birthday,
he had invited a few friends to celebrate but everything had been orderly
and at 3 a.m. they all had gone to the drugstore for coffee, after which
he had returned. In the morning, the super had waited and waited for
him to come out so she could clean, but when his pupils began arriving
and he still wasn't out, she had forced the door. There she found him,
all dismembered, everything blood-spattered.

It was then I suddenly thought of the apartment. Would she rent it to me? She recognized me, she said she'd like for me to have it but she couldn't even show it, the police still had the keys. I told her, "I'll take it sight unseen."

So we moved in, and when we did many people said, "Aren't you nervous, living in a place where a man was murdered?" Marchand was the first to answer: "No, because you can look around and see that this man must have been a marvelously-spirited person. He had a lot of taste. We don't even dream anyone was murdered here." Marchand was correct—and, so happy that we had our own world there, I did not begrudge it. Not one bit. There we were for three years, and everybody came to see him.

One was Gurdjieff, who came with five of his staff people. Gurdjieff wasn't supposed to be able to speak English but he did. He looked at Marchand and said Marchand had learned to live with his illness because he didn't look one ounce wasted. He had a full double chin and good color in the face.

To me, Gurdjieff said, "Why don't we have a place of yours? It's no good without one, no good." I explained that I couldn't leave Marchand, I had no one to nurse him. At that, Gurdjieff reached into his packet and gave me a little package, saying, "Now! Get somebody to care for him and find a place!" In the package was five hundred dollars to get a nurse. Added to the help I was getting from my brother, David, we lived on it for over a year.

Such visits Marchand received lying there like a king, enjoying himself and not dreaming he was going to die. Stefansson was going off for two years to teach in Mexico and South America. He said, "When I come back, I'll find Marchand either dead or in a hospital, being operated on." It happened exactly that way. When Stefansson returned in 1949 Marchand was in the hospital for a third operation. Stef called and said, "Before you tell me anything about Marchand, let me guess. He's dead, or he's in the hospital after a second or a third operation." I said, "Yes. He's in the hospital. He's a victim of experimenting on himself with his ideas."

But after Marchand came back to Grove Street from the hospital, again the good things I had taken from him stood me in good stead. It was a chilly, drizzly autumn night but various people were coming to see me and Marchand, including a woman who once had been a patient of his. Sick as he was, he examined her and noted she had a very bad cold. He told her, "I want you to go home immediately and get to bed." The woman had no umbrella, so I offered to walk her to the subway station, leaving a visiting Mexican friend of ours, Chiquita Rivera, to watch Marchand.

Near the station, as we were crossing the street, a car came and hit me, knocked me down. I was lying there bleeding, but thinking that Chiquita must leave to catch a train, and that Marchand will be alone. As police and a crowd surrounded me, I said, "Just take me across the street to the drugstore, they'll fix me up." But voices called out, "No, no, you must be X-rayed, and any minute you're liable to pass out."

Who faints when they're still able to be involved in what needs doing? I was able to give them the phone number to call Chiquita, so she could get somebody else in and not miss her train. Meantime, I let the police send me to St. Vincent's hospital but only for emergency bandaging of my forehead, after which I went home.

Next morning, when they took me to another hospital, they found a cracked right shin bone and some concussion, but no breaks. Yet they made me remain at the hospital. After five days I insisted I must leave to look after Marchand.

One of the doctors said, "It's ridiculous for you to leave now. You may think your husband will die if he's left alone, but if you leave you may be asking to die, too." They didn't comprehend how, with the things I took from Marchand's techniques and from my mother's, nature can be helped to heal.

Well, I threatened to escape. Finally Joe Julian, that big, tough actor friend of mine, he helped me persuade them and came to take me home. He told them, "This is one woman who'll get sicker lying here than being where she thinks she ought to be." So they gave me crutches, saying I must use them for weeks, that even with use of the crutches the shinbone injury might in time make a cripple out of me. I said no, I will leave that to nature.

I never used the crutches. When I got home, I went straight to Marchand's bed, I made myself stand on the healthy side of my foot, and I went on with my interest in him. And to this day, I have experienced no serious after-effects, I merely added special sensitizing of that leg to my regular morning things. Of course I also believe in the role of a spiritual law which many church people talk about but don't practice, that if you give to others it comes back one way or another in goodness to you. I believe that, in proving to whatever High Intelligence there is that I was really interested in helping this man, Marchand, the healing came to me, too.

That shouldn't be called Christian Science, either. Christian Science involves a God upstairs—outside somewhere. I'm talking about the universal intelligence inside, the God within. The cure for many things is in two of those centers Gurdjieff spoke of, the head and the heart.

But Marchand had gone too far. Within two weeks, there in that little basement flat, he closed his eyes one day for good. I had moved him for a little bit to where he could see the moonlight shining. He said, "As long as that is there, what's to worry?" Later, as I said, he reached for my hand. "You're still my woman." And he died. Such obscurity for a great man. But I will not say he went tragically because he wasn't recognized. He was one man to whom recognition, so-called, was not a compliment. Quite the contrary, quite the contrary.

We had talked of cremation. He had recalled how it was with Rose, my shirtwaist sister. When she had died, years earlier, her husband Leonard Abbott had timidly suggested it might be nice to have Rose cremated and her ashes scattered in Bronx Park, near where they lived and where he used to take her in her wheelchair. When Leonard made that suggestion, I was exalted. He was just thinking it, as an intellectual dream; he said he didn't imagine my mother would approve.

Not rather have her dear daughter near a brook in the park, where little blue flowers grow, than put in some dark hole? As soon as I told Mother, she was approving, and the thing was done. We went to the very place where Leonard used to take Rose on nice days. A little, freckled boy with red hair was playing down at the bottom of the ravine, where we were scattering the ashes. He said, "What flowers are you planting there?"

And so with Marchand. Scatter him on the bridle path in Central Park, he said, and I believe it was not so much anti-people as because of his belief in that feeling that animals always have but that man with his brain sometimes inhibits.

After Marchand died, I was in a bad state. I had to sleep alone. I am not a woman to sleep alone. Yet, for the first time in 35 years, people who were coming to see me were not staying until all hours. I began to phone people to come and stay overnight with me. One day the daughter of Berkeley Tobey—Judy—who had come from Provincetown to New York and was working for Brentano's, came to see me. While we were having coffee the telephone rang several times. Each time it was a friend to ask how I was, but when I asked each of them to come and stay with me the answer was always, "Oh, Marie, I'm so sorry, I just can't."

Finally this girl, this Judy, said to me, "Marie you know I've loved you since I was six years old. Well, I have a drastic thing to say to you. I would like to see you commit suicide. To think that you have to hang on the phone and beg people to come stay overnight with you—and they refuse! I don't want you to live such a life, you who people sought out for their needs."

I thought to myself, here's this kid forty years younger than I am, she's giving me a challenge. I shall accept it. To go on grieving, to try to collect debts of friendship when the secret of my giving was that I was nourished by the giving, is not a healthy way. So to her I said,

"Judy, you aren't shocking me. You are giving me a challenge. I will look into resuming the caravan. I will return to life."

12. Back in Action

Marie was now almost 65. Was there a place for her in the Village of 1950, a need among old friends and young discoverers to match the intensity of her need for serving them? Her answer had to be yes, else she felt she would shrivel up and blow away. But she went through the motions of pondering the scene.

Amid shrill tabloid-press cries about a "beat" generation and another passing of real Bohemia, Marie saw the presence of a core group with the same old hungers. Pizza pie and espresso coffee were new, but a continuing surge of artsy-craftsy shops, theatre groups and little galleries in the Village and also eastward toward the old New York ghetto suggested to Marie the continued need of food for the communal spirit.

Perhaps "Friends of the Romany Marie Tavern" could regroup to help her get back into action. This loose-leaf organization had come into being in 1939, when Marie's chronic financial woes threatened to make her 25th Village year her last. The result, then, had been a grand anniversary-benefit banquet, attended by 300 persons and staged at the Hotel Breevort, the cherished Fifth Avenue Village hostelry whose days also were numbered.

A prime mover in this was explorer Joseph Robinson. He had written to Marie in mid-1939, "All your friends will be one voice in declaring that your place must not close. Men and women all over the world think of the Village in terms of the unique atmosphere of your place, and with enduring memories of you that no other tavern or personality in the Village could inspire. Close Romany Marie's and for many of us you may as well close the Village.

"Only recently, Lowell Thomas was asking when we might plan another evening at 'Marie's,' one such as we gave for Philip Plant, Lady Hubert Wilkins, Dr. Stefansson, Peter Freuchen, Louise Boyd, Dr. Walter Granger, Bob Bartlett, Mr. and Mrs. Thomas E. Dewey, and many others. So you see, you must carry on."

Perhaps, Robinson audaciously suggested, Marie should even consider a larger place and a promotional campaign, to begin reaping a more appropriate financial return. Robinson was joined by a group of other Marie fans in disseminating an invitation to join a "Friends of —" group whose members would lunch, dine and sup at the Romany Marie Tavern and give parties there that might otherwise be arranged elsewhere. Those who signed the 1939 invitation put the year of their first acquaintance with the "Tavern" or with Marie:

Holger Cahill 1912
Henry Alsberg 1913
Niles Spencer 1913
Charlotte Carr 1915
Witter Bynner 1917
Arthur Ficke 1917
Rockwell Kent 1918
Kyra Markham 1918
Stuart Davis 1920
Muriel Draper 1920
Antonio Salemme 1920
Joseph Robinson 1923
Vilhjalmur Stefansson 1923
Paul Robeson 1924
Hubert Wilkins 1924
H. Binga Desmond 1926
Jackson Phillips 1930
Mary Sachs 1930
Arthur Frank 1931
Walter Granger 1934

"Most of those who were consistent patrons, whether 24, 14 or 4 years ago, are friends of Marie's and believers in the spirit for which her Tavern stands," they said in their brochure. "This, then, will be a distinguished roster, many of the names prominent in art, letters and theatre, with a few conspicuous in business and other walks of life." But they had remained true to Marie's dislike for pandering to success.

"Failure to become 'distinguished,' frequently the result of bad breaks, is also due in many cases to such faults of the success mechanism as modesty, unselfishness, lack of ruthlessness," the group wrote. "Those who value most the spirit of the Romany Marie Tavern are, on the average, less impressed with 'success' than almost any other group with a common bond anywhere in New York.

"The friends of the Romany Marie Tavern will be those who belong there, whether or not they belong also in a Hall of Fame. The list will not include famous people who have been there just a few times, perhaps merely as guests or sightseers."

A typical response came from humorist Fred C. Kelly: "Would I join the Friends of Romany Marie? That's the very thing I dote on doing. I got acquainted with her—though she didn't exactly know it—during the European War (the other one, back in 1918) when I was compelled to stay in New York on a war job and was in desperate need of a restaurant that was not standard and forbidding. I have considered myself a friend of Romany Marie ever since. Yes, you can count on me!"

Despite the cautious exclusivity, the December 1, 1939 Brevoort testimonial that became the "Friends" prime agenda went into the records as a banner event. With artist Rockwell Kent presiding, one highlight was an evocative dance by Ruth St. Denis. She performed behind the head-table chairs, without benefit of costume or sets, but according to some of those who saw her she succeeded in creating a terpsichorean image of Marie's earth-mother qualities.

Author-journalist Eugene Lyons, one of many speakers, said, "When I was a kid and came to the Village, it was Romany Marie's. And the other day my daughter telephoned me and said, 'I've been to Greenwich Village for the first time, and guess where I went? Romany Marie's.'" And singer Kate Smith did a CBS radio broadcast from the dinner, in which she spoke of "warm, vivid Romany Marie, a name synonymous with giving."

But that was 1939—and Marie's proceeds were more emotional than material. Like Marchand's dodging the railroad men alleged to have been interested in his instant coffee, she had continued to fail to cash in on her fame. Now, it was 1950. Marie discovered that many of those who still survived among the Friends of the Romany Marie Tavern were either eager or solicitous, but she proved incapable of crystallizing among them sufficient financial backing to establish a twelfth Romany Marie Tavern.

Undaunted, she fell back upon an alternative that taxed her pride but kept her in action in her beloved milieu.

She became a sort of reigning Character in Residence. For the next ten years, beginning at the El Charro on Charles Street, she held court in a series of small Village bistros owned and operated by others. Often, the publicity described her as a "partner," but the truth was she sat through the evenings for not much more return than the price of her own dinner, coffee and cigarettes.

Only her brother David's generosity made possible her living in a succession of mostly dreary rooms which she occupied after finally deciding to move from the flat where Marchand had died. Frequent moves and shared telephones, combined with the absence of a Romany Marie Tavern, made it frustratingly difficult for out-of-town admirers to locate her. Sometimes, she even wondered why she had resisted the early offers of John Sloan's wife, Dolly, and others to leave the Village for Santa Fe, New Orleans or San Francisco.

Yet, periodic bursts of press attention kept her always-ready ministrations in demand by a significant hard core of old admirers and introduced them to a new set of young people. Hosts of young Villagers regarded her only with friendly curiosity, as a museum piece, but others found a timelessness in her wisdom and her stubborn insistence that sex and the body had been unveiled in the Village numerous times before and shouldn't now be made the center of a four-letter-word ideology. Sometimes, press notes about Marie stemmed from nothing more than her Village strolls, as in 1951 when a reporter talked with Sybil Jacobsen, daughter of English playwright Frank Sutton-Vane and wife of Norman Jacobsen. Mrs. Jacobsen was quoted as saying that, while walking through the Village with the wife of painter Guy Pene duBois, she saw "a wonderfully strong and beautiful face among the passersby. Romany Marie: I never saw her before, but Norman had painted her for me—in words. I knew her at once!"

Another such splash of attention came in 1957 when the *Village Voice* published a three-part series on Marie, and it elicited a response from Katherine Anne Porter.

It was in many ways a predictable response, given Porter's own unconventional Village background. In a later interview with the *Washington Post*, she recalled her madcap bohemian youth: she'd worn only miniskirts and knee socks in the mid-twenties and painted her kneecaps with sunflowers, daisies, clown faces and even Picasso designs.

The gentle author of *Pale Horse, Pale Rider* and *Ship of Fools* could not understand how she had happened to be among the Village few who had missed going to Marie's in the twenties, but then went on to recall how she finally had met Marie at Woodstock. It was a summer, she wrote, when the placid country atmosphere there was being disrupted by the insane, drunken rages of a novelist named Leonard Cline, who later shot to death his best friend and eventually was himself found dead in bed. These rampages, she said, "made life so devilish for most of us—there were about a dozen of us scattered around in the barns and icehouses and chicken coops as well as the main house—that I was on the point of giving up and leaving, when Romany Marie came up to spend a weekend with Cline and his wife.

"Marie was a swarthy, weathered, beautiful woman in early middle-life, calm and smiling and wearing her gypsy clothes as if she were born to the pattern, though everybody knew she was no gypsy, she said so herself. She just liked the idea of gypsies and decided to look like one.

"She lent color and a kind of reality to the vaguely formless existence of the farm, and in the evening we all built a fire and sat around it singing, believe it or not, until Cline got off on his mad high horse, when we scattered, and Romany Marie came to my place, the ice-house, to spend the night.

"I barred the doors and put out the lights, and Leonard Cline careened and howled around the place, and beat on the doors demanding that we let him in, for a wearisome while. Romany Marie listened to the din in perfect calmness, but I was quite exhausted after several hours of it; and she suggested that while Cline was beating on the front door, we should take our cot mattresses, thin little rags they were, out the back door, and take refuge in the woods up the hill. We did this, running and hauling our mattresses after us. We sat there, in the moony woods, hearing the poor madman shouting and raging below, until at last his wife persuaded him to go in their house. We smoked and talked a while about all sorts of things, and of Cline Romany Marie said, 'Oh, we must pity him. He is so much more unhappy than he can possibly make anybody else!'

"We finally slept, and the next thing I knew, it was daylight, I smelled cigarette smoke, heard the rustle of Romany Marie's four or five long ruffled gay-colored skirts, and saw her stamping out her live cigarette with her bare foot. She rubbed her hands over her face, smoothed her hair, shook out her skirts, and was ready to go. I felt terribly disheveled, which I was, and could hardly wait to make our breakfast coffee.

"Odd thing is, I don't remember anything more about this episode, or how it ended, but Romany Marie and I were friends after that. This must have been in 1926 or '27; I went later to Bermuda, back to Mexico, and on to Europe, and didn't see her for nearly 10 years. But when I went back, she remembered instantly, and we talked again about our flight to the woods, and Romany Marie said, with the transfiguring power of her memory: 'Oh, weren't we like two nymphs pursued by a satyr?' It is now years again since I have seen her, and I hope to see her soon, for I know she will be sitting there with that marvelous air of repose and gentle confidence, not changed at all, and I will say, 'Marie, Marie, Marie, do you remember that night in the woods?' and she will say—but of course I don't know exactly the words she will speak, but she will smile her same smile, and remember."

Each such warm bath of nostalgia pleased Marie only to the degree that it released new freshets of involvement for the days she now was living. She could no more rest on her laurels than she could eat off them. "It's always today," she said, again and again. An unflagging, almost desperate adherence to this maxim saw her through yet another remarkable decade, surviving a heart attack, an assault that almost ended in rape, and worst of all, a protracted testing of her belief in people. In 1960, Marie looked back upon these years.

Marie:

The minute I asked myself the question after Marchand's death of why not again—why not resume my function?—I lost disillusionment. I became terribly interested. I could see that yesterday's various revolutions and languages were taking new form but were not, in fact, any different. Human nature remained the same, stupidities remained the same; wasn't it mostly the tempo of change that was creating the confusion? I would have to be easy, to discover what I had to meet this new tempo.

But where and how? While I was sitting, trying to think out ways, some friends were asking, "Marie, why go looking for a new load? Aren't you tired of the same old thing—of being a regular service station for people?" They astonished me. Thank heaven I had that little Judy's challenge to keep me on track. I told them, "You may as well say you are tired of life. Life's demands are repetitious, too, if that's how you want to look at it. You have to eat, you have to sleep, you have to make love, you have to function—always the same old thing, unless you reach out for the evolving interest, the revolutionary interest that is always there."

So along came a Rose Miller, who owned and operated a women's apparel shop in the Village, an expensive shop. I knew her more as a patron than as a close friend, but she had shown a very generous helping hand while Marchand was ill. His departure had touched her deeply. She said to me, "Marie, I'm eating often in a little restaurant on Charles Street, the El Charro. I think they would be interested in arranging for you to go and sit there each night, and meet your friends old and new, and get a little percentage from it. The owner's a very sympathetic little Spanish woman." Well, it was a decision between keeping myself isolated forever from all but those who wished to come see me in the flat, or going where those still anxious to see me could find a place.

So I went. The owner, named Maria, she and her husband, Garcia, knew about me, and she agreed to publicize my presence to my friends and to pay me a little percentage, especially on the drinks. But the first week I was there, I discovered they liked to close the place very early each night, they felt because they opened in the afternoon they should close early. Just about the time I used to begin, they closed. My friends, especially those who drank a little, did not come in at such hours.

This presented a handicap. So shortly after I started, this Maria took me out for dinner on her day off and told me the bad news: not having enough of my friends coming in during those hours, she couldn't afford to pay me a percentage. The food alone didn't warrant a percentage, and my friends didn't drink much. I could continue to have my dinners there at El Charro, but no money.

I said to myself, well most people no longer need to see me. I no longer have to give them what they used to get, all they need to do is get together in their own homes and remember the old times. But a few of those who were coming argued with me, they said, "By God, you don't realize how many there are who still have something to see you for. You still have something, kid, just give it a chance."

I discovered they were correct, in the most marvelous way. It happened to be the month of my birthday, and on the seventeenth of May I walked into the El Charro without having notified anybody. This is because I never went with this business of a birthday once a year. Each new day you're born again, there is a birthday every day. Every day you start afresh and—you may not notice it sometimes—there always is a little, little new thing that hasn't been seen before.

Well, I walked into the El Charro, and it was a garden of flowers. Flowers and cards to me. It was a big party, with Niles Spencer, and Varese, ever the French romantic. There were Holger Cahill, and Stuart Davis, and John Sloan who announced that I looked in my happiness fine and handsome, and I reminded him there was a time when he would have at least said beautiful, not handsome. Also there was some explorer, he had just returned that day from years in Brazil, he didn't know my place was closed and he had gone to look for me on Grove Street, he brought the most magnificent bouquet and a bottle of champagne. At last he was back home, he said.

Another of my friends there that night was a young woman scholar, Eloise McCaskell, who had collaborated with Stefansson. At that time, she happened to be working for a man in California who was writing his autobiography and was sending her the material to edit. It was none other than the great Lee DeForest, who invented the radio tube and also had something to do with the beginnings of television, he had lived in the Village 25 years before and used to come to my places. Well, when she arrived at the party, it was very excitedly, saying, "Marie, look what I've received from Lee DeForest!"

She read me a letter she had gotten from him that very day. It told of a great banquet to be given for him in a few days at the Waldorf Astoria by 4,000 of his fellow engineers. He was elated about it, he wrote, he and his wife who was a movie actress from the silent film days were coming. So, he told this girl, the night before the banquet—and mind, I hadn't seen or heard from this man in 25 years—he wished her to determine where Romany Marie was located so he could arrange to have a dinner there. She told me that he wanted the people at this dinner to include all the women whom he'd loved or to whom he'd proposed marriage in his younger days.

Naturally, I felt elated about this man remembering me. I called over Maria, the El Charro owner, and said, "Look, the dinner this great man wishes can be staged here. It will entail some fine publicity for the place." She looked at me and said, "Yes, but how long is he going to keep the tables? People like that have a habit of lingering too much, and I will need the tables."

It was a little shock to me. Poor dear, she felt she had to have turnover, she was in the restaurant business, not in the venture of maintaining a center for lingering tempo. I said, "But Maria, do you know what this means? One night he gives a party here, and the next night 4,000 engineers give him a banquet at the Waldorf." Nothing moved her. She said, "What time will they come? You know we close early." I said, "Well, that night you could close a little later." Recalling how important it was that we never watched the clock in my places, people talked until five o'clock in the morning, this conversation with Maria took a little off my enthusiasm. But I promised to see to it they wouldn't stay too late, and we went ahead with it.

On the same night that Lee DeForest and his group came, there was also in the place some kind of prizefighter, eating. The owners were very excited about him, but not about Lee. That same night it also happened through me that Ruth Bryan, the granddaughter of William Jennings Bryan, came in with her husband. In my place, that would have added up to one of the most animated of nights, but the way at El Charro was to worry about how long the tables would be kept.

Still, we had a wonderful evening. DeForest, who was then still working on inventions at the age of 79, was very much alive and very amusing, making deft remarks to his old loves who were there. His very beautiful actress wife announced she was going to write her own book, *How To Be Married To A Great Man*. Another of my guests, my brother-in-law Leonard Abbott, said he would help her, and they became very chummy. The whole thing was so intimate and wonderful that DeForest almost left without settling the bill, it was that homey, but he turned back and took care of it. It was quite a sum that he left there.

Anyway, it was part of the new wine for my spirit. As time passed, little by little the El Charro was kept open later until finally they were emancipated enough to stay open until about midnight. More of my friends got into the habit of coming in, and the result was I found myself sitting there for about three years. The owners seemed to become quite attached to me, were wonderful in the way they fed me, dined and wined me, took care that I didn't have to go home alone, and did everything to make me comfortable. They were different from my way, but good. And if it wasn't bringing me any money—well, I always said I never liked money, and if I say I don't like you, you stay away. So I was learning too late that money, well-used, can be a kingdom. I was still hoping it would kiss and make up with me.

Meantime, with the establishing of the El Charro arrangement, I came to the recognition that I should no longer cling to the place where Marchand died. There was a little mouse in the flat now, we never had even one mouse before Marchand closed his eyes. Somebody said if I moved I should take the mouse with me. But with or without mouse, I should move. It's wonderful to live alone, perhaps, but it's also nice to have someone around to tell you how wonderful it is to live alone. If it couldn't be with another man, all right it should at least be with some young people, if possible.

The most amazing thing developed. I had an opportunity to take with two young girls one of the apartments in the Studio Building on Tenth Street. Not only was it the first Village building ever designed especially for artists, and had housed Winslow Homer and Sargent and what's-his-name who painted Washington Crossing the Delaware, but old friends of mine had lived here, such as Stirling Calder and his boy, Sandy Calder, who created the mobile.

But the day for moving came, to leave the basement on Grove Street for the studio on Tenth, how was I going to move all the big things, like the tables? Well, here is where another of those things happened that made people insist I had some kind of mystic divination, that I could sense how things will turn out. I agree it happened too often to be only coincidence.

A knock came on the door and I opened it to see this huge bulk of a man. Dickie Murphy, who was there, sits petrified. Dickie was a very talented fellow, but a homosexual, a little chap, he was simply petrified. The man asked directions, I forget to where. I was tempted to tell him to go away, but he looked in and saw all the confusion and asked if I was moving. He has a car, he said, he can help take some things. Will I let him take some things?

A big, powerful man—Abe from the Bronx, he called himself, a wrestler or a prizefighter or something. To get to the point, he made two or three trips with his car, he picked up the big tables like they were matchsticks, and I was moved!

I asked him, "Can I do something for you?" He smiled. "I can tell you've done things for people, it's time something was done for you." He put all the stuff into the new place, and he was gone! I never saw him again. But I had the moral: there's no energy ever lost. You go on helping people as best as you can, and then all of a sudden, when you need help, out of nowhere comes an Abe from the Bronx.

Maybe this kind of episode is why somebody like Laura Benet never took a step, hardly, without asking me. Once she asked me about her taking a trip to England to develop some writing projects. No, I said to her, the English are puritanical, you should better consider doing more of your writing in biographies about actors and on adolescence. She did that, and she made a nice success of it.

Laura really was part of a story of my life since Marchand's death, even though we first met in the early twenties. She was sent to me at that time by Lola Ridge, the poetess, to ask my advice. A shy, almost frightened young woman, Laura came to my door and asked me some sort of question without even introducing herself. I said, "Who are you?"

"Well, I'm Laura Benet. I was sent to you by Lola Ridge, a very dear friend of mine and yours too." All the time she was acting very shyly, careful not to be seen by the people inside the place. I asked her to come in, but she refused, she wanted to speak to me outside. I don't recall now what her question was, but when I gave her what answer I could she took it very eagerly and hurried away. From then on, regularly, she would call me or call on me to ask advice, but always she remained anxious to refrain from facing the people in the place.

On questioning Lola Ridge, I learned that Laura quite naturally worshipped her two brothers, Stephen Vincent and William Rose Benet, and she was terribly chary about having people talk to her about them. I, upon learning all this, let her be as she was.

Years and years passed, she continued to see me in the same way until the changes came in my life—my closing the last place, Marchand's death. Then, she began to walk in and visit me, and—shy as she still was—even to be a little more relaxed with people I introduced her to.

Still more time passed. Lola Ridge died, Laura's brothers passed on, it seemed as if she felt I was the only one left for her to ponder things with. I found her most solicitous and sympathetic with my sadness and with the changes taking place in my life. She would be willing to rouse herself in the night and do things to ease my loneliness. I noticed she would also do such things for others. A very selfless and grand person. I saw how she was always eager to put over her poems and books, always humble in her quest for the right ways to go.

Suddenly, it dawned on me that she had gone through a long, long span of time without being talked about or noticed as she deserved. This came from her modesty, her care to avoid blowing her own horn or mentioning all the things she had been doing for others. I saw in a flash that truly she was one of those persons whose left hand does not know what the right hand is doing—or, more correctly, doesn't permit it to know. The thought came to me that except for her writing, which was very much Laura Benetish, people knew too little about her. I felt that, for posterity, there should be a bust made of her, and to my mind came the name of Tony Salemme whom I hadn't seen in years. I promptly telephoned him.

As he spoke about being so happy to hear from me, I asked if he ever had heard of Laura Benet. He jumped to that name, saying, "No, but I knew her late brother, William, very well. We were good friends." I told him a few things about Laura that would put the focus on her, and he asked me to bring her to his studio uptown. She proved willing, especially when she learned that Salemme had known one of her brothers, and to my agreeable surprise when he said he wished to do a bust of her, Laura promptly agreed to go and pose as much as he needed.

So a beautiful bust of Laura Benet was born. Either the Poetry Society, of which Laura has been a very important member for almost half a century, will buy it, or somebody else will, but there it is, done in bronze. It is a thing for posterity that I feel was a significant element for me this late in my life.

The same thought involved me as I moved into the Tenth Street studio, to share it with two young girls: Why should my lack of a place inhibit what I have left to give? Somebody else's center, a studio, a two-by-two room, a boat, a radio station—what does the environment matter if there is a need that calls upon me to make it like my place? To be needed by some part of the world one lives in, to help in somebody's confusion or suffering, to have an occasional taste of the wonders of nature—what more is there?

So, to these girls in the studio, I said, "Look girls, this is a studio, a place with a rich atmosphere, it's a shame to waste it. I wish you could make a little cultural center of it where people could get together and discuss things." They say well, that's fine, and before I knew it they began to bring in other young people. They'd go around saying, "Guess who's living with us?"

They gathered, and as a general principle I observed that it's not I who attracted them but the Village. For the first time in 35 years I could be detached, because I could see they weren't waiting for me to make the Village, they were making it themselves. The need for getting together still operated productively, and when they did get together, what did they care about me, about Romany Marie of the past, they were just starting their adventure.

But every now and then they'd kind of perk up their ears because of my connection with things that were current, such as Bucky Fuller's work or Mark Tobey's paintings. This opened the way to my responding to their need for coordination of their restlessness, a coordination which many of them still lacked.

I discovered that I could meet, with my love, the task of telling those just then starting how to steer their way.

13. The Queen is Dead

One night in February 1961, distressing word reached Laura Benet, whom Marie so many times had mentored and whom she had arranged for John Sloan to paint. Marie was ill.

"I sent over a nurse, even though Marie insisted she only had bronchitis," Ms. Benet said. "Next morning the nurse telephoned to say that Marie was in a coma, from which she didn't recover." She was 77—or thereabouts.

To the accompaniment of that *Village Voice* headline that bespoke the death of a Queen and that said, "There is no other," a standing-room-only memorial service was held in a West Side branch of Manhattan's Cooke Funeral Homes.

David Rout's elder son, Lee Rout, remembered that he first reserved the smallest funeral home room but finally ended up with the largest, on the strength of the numbers of people who planned to attend. The neighborhood was uptown, leading one woman present to murmur, "Imagine Marie in a place like this!"

The secular service began with a reading of verse from the Bahai movement that Marie had embraced in the twenties and that had established her as such a supporter nationally that many Bahai members attended. Among Marie's old friends who spoke was curator Monroe Wheeler of the Museum of Modem Art, who said, "She loved the little ones as much as the great ones. She intensified joy when luck was running high. She wrote a vital page in the cultural history of New York."

Stuart Davis, also there, added to the talk of later-celebrated people who were fed in belly and spirit by Marie. He named the likes of O'Neill, Hippolyte Havel, George Bellows, radical editor Max Eastman and muckraker Lincoln Steffens.

And then there was author Konrad Bercovici, a Romanian-born author known for having collected a million dollars for plagiarism from the makers of Charlie Chaplin's movie, *The Great Dictator*. Bercovici spun a story he attributed to Anatole France about the centipede who couldn't get out of bed after another insect asked him which of his hundred legs he put down first. Said Bercovici, "Romany Marie walked on all the hundred feet she had—which was her heart."

On hand at the service with those survivors of the "great days of Bohemia" were disciples of more recent vintage, including Geoffrey Vincent, a senior writer from the Sunday *New York Times*. Vincent looked at Marie in her open coffin.

"She looked very peaceful, with a faint smile," he wrote later in a letter. "She was wearing a rose-and-gray dress with a blurry print and she had on her bracelets and rings. A woman in line in front of me bent down and kissed her. I walked into the corridor which was also beginning to fill with people even before the announced calling hour, and I heard a man in black say to someone who must have complained about the facilities, 'We gave her the biggest room we've got.'

"I went down to the lobby and out into the sunshine. There wasn't a room big enough no matter where they looked."

By the time the 21st century dawned, few were left who remembered Marie, except kinfolk or legacy perpetuators of the likes of Buckminster Fuller or Stuart Davis. Those who do survive tend to need a mental jog to remind them of the woman who was a touchstone for them in their times of early struggle.

Indeed, that otherwise formidable 1994 *Culture and Counterculture* volume on Greenwich Village old and new went for the skeptical, superficial description of Marie in a boxed text that accompanied a reproduction of her portrait by John Sloan.

It referred to her as the operator of "a series of Village eateries" who had a "guise as a bohemian restaurateur." With nary a mention of her role as a special mentor and benefactor of struggling artists, writers, players and explorers, the book's sources waved Marie off as "the doyenne of cozy Village eateries." She was described as "a former acolyte of the anarchist Emma Goldman" and portrayed as a poseur whose accented "ripening Romanianism" increased for curious tourists.

But not excepting the commercial and heavily publicized Elaine's, nobody in the remembering group could recall a sustaining personality on hand to give spirit, rather than a beer or a drink. There was no memory of a host driven by his or her own interest in the aspiration of others, rather than by his or her own role as a restaurateur, or his or her own ambitions as a painter, actor, dancer, writer or director.

There were quaint exceptions. Into the opening decade of this 21st century, the longtime Village resident who conducted neighborhood tours featuring Village ghosts starred Marie as one of the attractions.

Jeanne Keyes Youngson, a leader of the "International Society for the Study of Ghosts and Apparitions," recalled having seen Marie in the 1950s, when no longer with her own place she held court for old friends at the El Charro Mexican restaurant on Charles Street.

"When I started my Village walks, in the early 70s, I met a lovely old lady, Alice something, nearly 100, who was a puppeteer," Ms. Youngson said. "She told me that Romany Marie's ghost had been 'seen' a few times by people who lived near the restaurant, still sitting at the same table. She said a British psychic had asked one of the owners about the ghost, but was assured that no such apparition existed.

"Still, the psychic did feel a presence, but he could not tell if it was that of a man or a woman."

Ms. Youngson added, "I haven't been to the restaurant for years, but I well remember Romany Marie at her table, and that she never seemed to be eating." So accurately, the ghost seeker felt Marie was there only to offer a serving role to those who came looking for it.

Even before Marie's death, MOMA's Dorothy Miller mused about what role there might be for a Marie and one of her centers.

As the proponents of a new Bohemia do aptly point out, years of shared economic or unrecognized struggle no longer beset the creators of new art forms in the degree they used to when the Village retained its Left Bank separateness. Some of the most obscure theatre groups and deviant-style artists now get what Miller called the Big Nod from *The New York Times* and often are quickly on their way to the Big Time.

Moreover, there is now on a broad basis across the country more and more of the healthy inclusion of homosexuals and racial minorities who used to be accepted only in the Village.

But what would Marie say about applying the "Bohemia" label to the marginal and the mundane? How would she react to those standards of a new, bourgeois Bohemia that might very well transform the lover character in *La Boheme* into a stockbroker high on Ecstasy and the heroine into a victim of AIDS?

Afloat in two generations of sexual experimentation and breakthrough creativity, Marie might very well cheer, yet frown at bohemianism turned middle-brow.

"Bohemia and bourgeois are two entirely different worlds and cannot ever be the same," she said in 1960, as she noted the changes already taking effect.

"To be bohemian means to treasure a lingering tempo, and what I am seeing among the young is the loss of a lingering tempo. I see human nature remaining the same, stupidities remaining the same, but a tempo of change is creating confusion, it is a tempo that does not go with Bohemia."

Marie was reminded of John Reed, whose own political bohemianism was popped into mainstream awareness by Warren Beatty with the film *Reds*. "John wrote of nights blazing with arguments uproarious," she mused, "but they were long nights, not like now punctuated by banal ra-ta-ta music and distracted by an urge for money and recognition."

Suppose from what Marie stubbornly envisioned as that Great American Beyond, that "Oshkosh or Hodge Podge" outside the Village, a new Marie is waiting to emerge?

Were one to appear, her very first, full-length spotlighting in *The New York Times* would come quickly and would lead a thinning chorus of old bohemians to cry havoc and run for the roachy kitchen.

In prose and poetry they might very well conclude that even a contemporary Marie could not recreate an oasis of undefiled Bohemia. In these times of prevailing two-way spillage between the Village and the off-off-off Broadways and Uptown, a Marie may be only a sweet memory—and what is here needs a name other than Bohemia.